PERSPECTIVES IN READING NO. 12

A New Look at Reading
in the
Social Studies

Compiled and Edited by

RALPH C. PRESTON
University of Pennsylvania

Prepared by a Committee of the
International Reading Association

RALPH C. PRESTON
Chairman of the Conference

International Reading Association
Newark, Delaware 19711

INTERNATIONAL READING ASSOCIATION

FOREWORD

THE IRA PERSPECTIVES CONFERENCES provide opportunities to discuss a wide range of significant issues and topics. This volume includes papers presented at the conference held in Washington in connection with the 1968 convention of the National Council for the Social Studies.

Ralph C. Preston planned the conference program to emphasize the role that reading might play in making social studies instruction more effective. Hence, the volume is of significance both to the social studies teacher and to the reading teacher.

The demands of society for developing higher levels of literacy, especially of critical thinking, are reflected in the papers concerned with controversial issues and learning through criticism. As a basis for critical reading and thinking, persistent problems relating to reading and the language arts, the vocabulary problem, and the role of primary source material are also considered. The result is a balanced volume reflecting the qualities of the conference itself which was well received, indeed.

In reading this volume, teachers will find topics and approaches significantly different from those ordinarily presented when discussing reading in the social studies. This fact in itself will make for worthwhile reading and insures the valuable contribution that a new look at reading in the social studies makes to the literature.

LEO FAY, *President*
International Reading Association
1968-1969

Contents

Reading and other Language Arts in Social Studies Instruction: Persistent Problems

Wayne L. Herman, Jr.
University of Maryland

There are numerous approaches to teaching the social studies. If we were to list and categorize these approaches, most of the categories would probably be representative of the areas of the language arts: listening, speaking, reading, and writing. This paper will identify from the research literature some of the urgent perplexities of teaching the social studies through the languages arts.

Children's Interests in the Social Studies

Although we know that children's interests vacillate, for the past few decades research on children's preference for subjects has consistently revealed some defects in social studies programs. As yet we do not know for sure what these defects are, although a lot of us have some notions. Perhaps this paper will merely add to the conjectures as it troubleshoots among the language arts. Two decades ago the investigation by Jersild and Tasch (47) told us something was wrong with the way social studies was being taught. On all grade levels pupils gave social studies a low ranking. One glaring inconsistency was noted. Whereas children in grades 4-6 ranked social studies first as the subject they liked the least, when they were asked which topics they would like to learn more about in school, they mentioned topics pertaining to social studies more than those of any other subject area. Each of the studies by Chase and Wilson (10), Curry (16), Herman (37), Holmes (43), and Rice (56) revealed children's low ranking of the social studies.

Balance Needed Among the Language Arts

While observing sixty-five hours of fifth grade social studies instruction during which five balanced visits were made to fourteen classrooms during a six-week unit (38), I found that children were reading only about 13 percent of the time. This small amount of time spent on reading raises some penetrating questions about the amount of scholarship going

1

on in classrooms. More appalling was the amount of time spent in writing, which was less than 2 percent of the total time. Total listening was 77 percent: listening to the teacher accounting for 12 percent; listening to pupils, 22 percent; and listening to teacher pupil conversations, 43 percent. The lopsidedness of listening-speaking when compared with reading and writing seriously needs correction.

You may question the validity of a teacher's behavior while being observed. Although a teacher may believe that she needs to do something of an active nature, such as talking, when a visitor is in the classroom, I would suggest that a teacher tends to do those things which will receive the approval of the visitor.

What is needed, it seems, is a balance between the inputs and the outputs of the communicative arts in social studies teaching. There are a few reasons for the desirability of balance. Listening and reading, as inputs, give pupils a background of information upon which to draw for output, that is speaking and writing. It is expected that a lack of input would seriously impair pupils' attempts at output. On the other hand, when output is minimal and, consequently, there is minimal reinforcement of ideas garnered from input, then we would expect that a sizable portion of the input, or learning, would be attenuated and much lost outright.

As my research shows, there is much output (speaking) and little input (reading). When this condition obtains, one can presuppose that the foundation of input on which output is based is flimsy and shaky. To put it simply, when reading activities are sparse, the speaking activities during the social studies deal with what children already know and the little that they have read about. One of the reasons for little emphasis on reading activities may be a direct result of the shocking disregard by teachers of their own personal reading, as found by Duffey (*20*). It is probable that teachers will promote little the activity in which they seldom participate. The disadvantage of speaking in the classroom is that only one pupil can contribute at a time. Writing affords each pupil simultaneously an opportunity to express his ideas and reinforce his learning.

Another reason for the plea for balance of language arts activities during social studies periods concerns the purpose of education, to teach all the skills of learning, all of the language arts. And one of the best ways to teach these skills is through a functional approach, such as that which the social studies provides. The supposition that teachers are spending time on speaking and listening activities because these need special attention appears faulty when we realize that generally pupils are better in speaking and listening then they are in reading and writing. Another respectable reason for balance is the motivating effect of a variety of learning activities which engage pupils actively.

Reading Conditions that Require Improvement

Because there is more research on reading than on other aspects of language in the social studies, it seems appropriate to direct this paper more to the area of reading than to the problems of the other language arts.

To begin, it might be well to look at the advantages that exist for reading in the social studies. Preston (55) writes in his crisp and forceful style that

> Reading has the power to carry the child further and deeper, in a given time unit, than any other educational medium. Moreover, he can analyze more thoroughly what he reads than what he hears from teachers or in discussion, or sees in films or in television. A passage in a book can be reread as and when needed by the child; he can compare passages for corroboration or to check seeming inconsistencies; he can stop for reflection when he wishes; he can often choose a time for reading that will fit in with his mood or personal needs; he can carry books around with him and can take school books home. The best of teachers, films, and guided trips have none of these advantages. Their ideas flow relentlessly and cannot be turned back at will like the pages of a book. Their pace may not be his. The book, in short, is the most adjustable, personally adaptable, and effective learning medium ever invented . . . .

For the child or high school student who reads proficiently, the printed page has no equal. Unfortunately, these highly skilled readers are often held back in their reading prowess by having to meet reading requirements that are beamed at the mean class intelligence. On the other hand, the average and less-able readers may believe that reading is overempasized in the social studies. Nearly all assignments require the ability to read, to locate information, to pinpoint the main idea, and then to understand it, remember it, and either write or recite it. It may seem paradoxical to these pupils—particularly pupils in the upper levels of the schools—that their learning outside of the school walls is balanced by different emphases whereas in school the written word has a prior lien on their academic time.

Although children are reading better today than they have ever read before, according to Gates (30), recent research indicates that grave reading problems exist in the social studies for nearly all except the few highly sophisticated readers. A look at pupil preferences for activities commonly used in social studies instruction shows that pupils are unfavorably disposed toward reading activities. Stewart's study (62) of children's choice in types of assignments clearly indicates that drawing and construction are top choices while reading and writing are generally disliked. When 398 sixth grade children ranked thirty-eight activities commonly used in the social studies, Foley (27) found that reading activities were unpopular.

When Penty *(53)* conducted interviews with poor tenth grade readers whose reading levels were as low as 4.3, she found feelings of hostility and inadequacy toward those courses in which reading the textbook is the dominant mode of learning. It ought to be mentioned that the findings of a study by Goebel *(32)* in the public schools of Topeka run counter to these studies. He found that reading for discussion has appeal for children of high, average, and low ability. Perhaps we should visit the classrooms in his study and find out what teachers are doing to make reading assignments attractive to children.

Reading instruction in the social studies is neglected. Maybe we would find that the teachers of the social studies in Topeka consider themselves teachers of reading. My experience in visiting classrooms shows that teachers of the social studies are predominantly not teachers of reading. In fact, it is easy to go one step further and say that teaching reading in the social studies appears to be related to the distance in grade level a teacher is from the primary grades: the further a teacher is away, the less he teaches reading.

Twenty years ago Gray *(33)* wrote ". . . teachers of different curriculum fields become concerned about reading problems as reading assumes importance in attaining the aims of teaching in those fields. Whereas the reading teacher lays the foundation of good reading habits, the content teachers play a highly significant role in extending and refining the reading efficiency of pupils in specific areas." A few years later Gray lamented that the responsibility of all teachers to teach reading had become the concern of no one.

It is imperative that social studies with its emphasis on reading be yoked with instruction in reading. The same procedure advocated by Betts *(7)* in his directed reading outlines for the basal reading story is the same mode, adjusted for variety and the composition of the class, that ought to be used for functional reading in the social studies: the teacher should motivate, build background, and pull out the new vocabulary and concepts. Who is better qualified to develop the vocabulary and concepts of the social studies than the teacher of the social studies? This question was the basis of an experiment by Herber *(36)* in teaching reading through the social studies in which significant gains in reading achievement were made.

Also, the procedure of setting purposes for reading ought to be considered before the silent reading. As far back as 1929 Washburne *(67)* pointed out that question-guided reading was superior to the generalized page assignment especially when the questions were posed before the reading and when the kinds of questions coincided with the kinds of understanding expected by the teacher. Following up the silent reading and enriching the reading complete Betts' directed reading outline.

Reading skills taught in the primary grades hardly vouchsafe the proficiency of reading skills in fifth or eighth or twelfth grades. Even with the better readers, unless reading skills continue to be taught, there can be a decline in reading competence. If anything, poor readers in the lower grades become worse readers in the higher grades. Reading skills, the most important of any skills taught in the schools, need to be taught and retaught throughout the grades. What better way can these reading skills be taught than in the functional setting of a content area, the social studies?

Even though the reading in social studies occurs for the most part in the elementary school classroom while out-of-class reading assignments characterize the junior and senior high schools, the basic problems for the reader regardless of his school level remain qualitatively the same. Quantitatively, reading perplexities increase for the junior or senior high school pupil. As a rule of thumb, if on an instructional reading level— with the teacher present to help the reader—readers ought to know 75 percent of the ideas in the passage and 90 percent of the vocabulary to avoid frustration, then higher limits are required for independent reading.

My observations of thirty-two teachers of above average, average, and below average classes for over one hundred hours of elementary school social studies instruction gave credence to the neglect of teachers to consider that instruction in reading and that in the social studies are inextricably related. Parenthetically, one must say that in the main these teachers used many exemplary activities to teach the social studies.

During these observations, it was common to observe a teacher telling his children to read several pages in the social studies textbook and then see him saunter aimlessly around the classroom. What did many of the pupils do while they were supposed to be reading? They read a few sentences or paragraphs and then gave up. They pretended to be reading until another activity began. If a child thought that he was not being watched, he might fondle a toy in his desk, doodle, look around the room, tie and retie a shoe lace, or interact with a friend—anything, except read. To be sure, some poor readers who are highly motivated may stick with it and get the jist of their reading. But there are few of these. What is there about reading that causes even average readers to give up? If one asked a boy why he did not read the social studies book when he was supposed to and if one had good rapport with him, the boy might answer reluctantly, "Aw, it's too hard. I just don't understand it." If they were honest, how many high school pupils would not give the same answer?

Research concerning reading in the social studies has some specific answers. It will be presented below in connection with reading conditions that require improvement.

Readability formulas are ignored by publishers.   Perhaps the malignancy of inaccurate readability as stated by publishers of social studies textbooks would appear more critical if we first took a quick glance at the basal reader, which many of us would agree should lead the way in matching readability to specific grade levels. In March 1963, Mills and Richardson (52) astonished the reading audience of *Reading Teacher* by citing an investigation in which they sent a questionaire to twelve major publishers of basal readers asking questions about the readability formulas the companies used for grading the readers. Only about half of the publishers responded, and half of these said they used no readability formulas but relied on the judgment of authors or educational consultants to determine the grade level of the basal readers. Using readability formulas, the investigators evaluated 200 basal readers and concluded that one-half of the books did not correspond with the intended grade. Such deplorable conditions for the basal reader, which is designed to build reading skills, portend even greater disparities for the readability of social studies textbooks.

For some time it has been well known that the textbook, instead of assisting pupils in acquiring knowledge, has impeded and discouraged many pupils in their studies. After reviewing the research on the adequacy of the textbook as a source and mode of teaching, about a year ago Hill (42) was prompted to write that there is solid evidence to confirm that the content area textbook as traditionally used, is less help and possibly more hindrance to the student than commonly assumed. In a review of textbook readability findings, Smith and Dechant (61) concluded that the textbooks in the content area may run one or two grades above their placement. Little wonder that average and above average pupils in addition to less endowed pupils experience difficulty with the printed word in the social studies.

Some specific studies in the social studies are pertinent. Arnsdorf (2) studied the readability of basal social studies materials used in the elementary school and found a progression of reading levels throughout the grades—as one might expect—but a wide range of readability within any one reader, the easier and harder reading occuring anywhere throughout the book. The readability of nearly half of the readers he examined was suited for a higher grade placement.

The encyclopedias that line the shelves beginning at grade three present similar difficulties to pupils. Edgerton (22) stated in his 1954 study that average reading levels of *World Book, Britannica Junior,* and *Comp-*

ton's encyclopedias were Grade 6, 7, and 8, respectively. Using the cloze test, Liske (*49*) completed a study this year of the readability of the 1967 edition of *World Book Encyclopedia,* the best known and most widely used encyclopedia. He concluded that teachers of grades four, five, and six ought to use encyclopedias with discretion, since only children of above average ability can use them successfully.

The benefit of paperbacks as supplementary reading materials is also highly suspect. After using the Spache formula to determine the readability of nineteen books of six different publishers, Maynard (*51*) advised that unless a controlled vocabulary is stated on the inside cover, paperbacks are undesirable for independent recreational reading for less able readers. Francis (*28*) came to a similar conclusion after reviewing studies of the readability of paperbacks. In his own investigation with Noall, Francis (*29*) determined the readability levels through use of the Flesch formula of over 250 ungraded paperbacks. The most important factor revealed in the study pointed up the need for more graded paperback literature to meet the needs of the student with varied reading levels, especially in high school.

Vocabulary load is excessive. Let us consider a specific problem of readability, that of vocabularly load. Two different handicaps confront pupils: first, vocabulary that is unknown to pupils; and second, vocabulary that contains familiar words that become incomprehensible in an unfamiliar setting (*60*). Russell and Saadeh (*58*) clarified this latter difficulty by their study of qualitative levels in children's vocabularies. They asked third, sixth, and ninth grade pupils to define a number of words and proceeded to classify the responses into one of three categories: concrete, functional, or abstract. For instance, they used the word "count." If the pupil's response was similar to "to find how many pennies are in your pocket," it was labeled concrete; "The number of things in a group" was classified functional; and abstract responses included "to say numbers in order—upward or downward." That concreteness and abstractions increased in the lower and higher grade levels, respectively, only serves to emphasize that the same words have different meanings to different people. Whereas the vocabulary in fifth grade social studies textbooks was more difficult than in sixth grade textbooks, Haffner (*34*) decided that textbooks on both levels contained excessive vocabularly loads.

At this point, one may be vacillating between two positions: "Yes, reading is a grave problem in the social studies," or "I doubt if the reading problem in the social studies is as serious as Herman thinks it is." The research evidence that we shall consider next ought to rid the reader of any doubts.

Some concepts are poorly taught.   Increased attention to concepts encountered in social studies materials seemed to begin after 1954 when Carner and Sheldon (9) reported that the problems in the development of concepts through reading consisted of problems dealing with concrete objects and processes and chronological, spatial, numerical, and social terms. In an investigation of the concepts found in basal social studies texts, Arnsdorf's findings (3) showed that pupils' understanding of concepts in social studies increased through the intermediate grades but that the differences in levels of comprehension were greater within rather than between grades.

- Two studies dealt with quantitative concepts in social studies textbooks. Lyda and Robinson (50) investigated second grade textbooks and reported that children of above average intelligence understood three-fourths of the quantitive concepts from the three social studies textbooks, average children understood a little less than half of the concepts, and below average children understood less than a fourth. Jarolimek and Foster (46) studied fifth grade children with grade placement scores in reading of 5.0 or above and found that children scored lowest in an understanding of concepts relating to indefinite reference of time. One conclusion of this study was that children of average or above average reading ability will be able to understand only about half of the concepts in social studies textbooks and below average readers, less than a third. Our rule of thumb is that unless pupils know 75 percent of the concepts on an instructional reading level or 90 percent of the concepts on an independent reading level, they will most probably be on a frustration level. Many above average readers read basal social studies materials on a frustration level.

There are more germane studies. Teachers need to be alert to indefinite references to time in textbooks, for these references are more numerous and more difficult than definite references to time. In a study of twenty-five books from four basal social studies series for the elementary school, Arnsdorf (4) found there were four times as many indefinite time terms, such as *old, day, century,* and *sometimes,* than there were definite time terms. In this same study, space terms such as *great, inland, miles, narrow, vast* were used more than time terms, and over 90 percent of the terms were classified as indefinite.

Suppose one were to ask, as Gill (31) did with elementary school children up through college students, the meanings of these words: *many years ago, in early days, until recently,* and *in ancient times.* The writer hypothesizes that there would be a range of answers for each expression. Gill found that these expressions were loosely interpreted at all grade levels, that a time sense and maturity were closely related, and some terms had no precise meaning for many students and caused much difficulty at the lower grade levels.

Both the vocabulary and the concepts in the reading assignments of the social studies should be discussed and clarified before the reading, not afterward as some school systems recommend. Discussing vocabulary and concepts after the silent reading may improve comprehension, but that approach hardly helps the pupil during his reading of the passage. Pupils are assisted with the meanings of new, hard, and unclear words and concepts when complete sentences are pulled and taught from the context.

We have several studies that validate a concept approach in the teaching of the social studies. Although maturity and concept understanding have a relationship, Davis (17) and Arnsdorf (5) in separate studies exploded the myth that for some concepts we have to defer instruction until children are "ready." The fourth, fifth, and sixth grade children in the investigation by Davis made significant gains in their understanding of time and space as related to geographical time zones. When Arnsdorf provided instruction in chronology to 563 sixth grade children with the use of time lines and biographical and autobiographical materials made by the children, time relationships were improved significantly.

Three other studies seem worth mentioning. Crabtree (15) successfully used an inquiry approach with children to teach concepts and generalizations in the social studies. She started with simple concepts and then extended those relationships to more complex conditions. Witt (70) combined reading instruction entailing outlining and drawing conclusions with a concept approach to teaching the social studies at the junior high school level and found that significant gains were made in both reading and in social studies. In case the reader has misgivings about his effectiveness in teaching conceptually, let me hasten to draw upon a finding of Carmichael's project (8) which stated that pupils taught conceptually, even by teachers without extensive conceptual training, made significant progress in geographical understandings.

Study skills are neglected.   Study skills are commonly ignored. Teachers wonder what they can do to help children with poor study skills. Since this is a reading problem, it seems appropriate to mention that Robinson (57) observed the reading skills that fourth grade children actually used in solving problems in the social studies. His findings were classified under two headings: *reading comprehension skills,* which included using experience or knowledge, defining the problem, grasping main ideas, reading for details, making inferences, drawing conclusions, comparing ideas, and understanding ideas; and *reference skills,* entailing selecting source material, using alphabetical order, locating specific information, using index and table of contents and guide words, and selecting appropriate meaning of words in the dictionary. Pupils should be given frequent practice with carrying out these tasks.

Disabled readers are not helped.   Even if social studies textbooks were improved and teachers of the social studies were teachers of reading, there remain the problems of the disabled and weak readers. In one fifth grade classroom, one of eight boys who sat in a row of desks apart from the rest of the class said, "We aren't given a social studies textbook because we can't read too well." When the writer asked what they did when the other children read, all of the boys nodded in agreement when one boy answered, "We just sit here. That's all. We just sit here all day, every day." This condition seems to exemplify the plight of the less able reader. To help these readers requires different modes which entail reading and nonreading activities. Matching an able child with a less able one has been highly successful. Duffey (*19*) suggests these ways that deal with reading: providing textbooks on lower levels of readability, easy trade books, junior news publications, textbook material rewritten by the teacher or by able pupils, experience charts, and study guides; and providing pupil specialties as advocated by Durrell and Savignano (*21*).

Speaking in the Social Studies

In a study of the use of language arts in fifth grade social studies, Herman (*37*) stated that the teacher and pupils were talking for 77 percent of the time. The three dominant activities occurring in these classrooms were "teacher questions—pupil answers" (12.3 percent), "pupil recites" (13.3 percent), and "teacher lectures with questions" (18 percent). A little more than three-quarters of the social studies lesson was devoted to speaking activities. This is a lot of time.

Inevitable questions are "What are they talking about all this time?" or "What kinds of questions does the teacher use to solicit children's responses?" Another line or inquiry would entail the amount of autocratic and democratic talk a teacher uses. Although there are numerous worthy trouble spots in this area of speaking, I will address only two topics of concern: the cognitive levels of talk during lessons and the verbal behavior of teachers during discussions.

In all probability, most of the speaking in social studies classrooms consists of a low level of talk. It is based largely on knowledge: facts, names, dates, specific accomplishments, exports and imports, and sequence of events. This talk relies heavily on memory. There are a few studies to substantiate this indictment. Floyd (*26*) studied the kinds of questions asked by primary grade teachers and found that 42 percent of the questions were at the lowest level of Bloom's *Taxonomy,* recall of knowledge. In a similar study, Davis (*18*) categorized questions used by student teachers—who, as everybody knows, ape the classroom teacher—in secondary school social studies and found that more memory questions were asked than all other kinds of questions combined.

The work by Clegg and his associates (*12, 13*) and by Taba (*64*) demonstrated that training of teachers in the use of higher order questions produced significant improvement. These studies also pointed out that the level of pupil response was at about the same level as their teacher's questions. When teachers engage on a low level of talk, so do children. When teachers use higher thought questions, the pupils follow suit. It is as simple as that.

The validation of the sequence of the categories of Bloom's *Taxonomy* and the appropriateness of each cognitive level to age, intelligence, and socioeconomic status of children offer promising frontiers of needed inquiry. Reports are beginning to appear in the literature of a few studies which attempt to raise the cognitive level of children's thinking. In addition to Taba's work (*64*) in Contra Costra County, California, which showed that below average children could indeed be taught to think, Hunkins (*45*) writes that the use of analysis and evaluation questions resulted in significantly greater gains in social studies achievement than the use of low cognitive level questions concerned with knowledge. When Clegg, Sebolt, and Benoit (*14*) gave children practice with the Bloom *Taxonomy* and later had the children prepare forty items for the unit test, 66 percent of the questions were at the "higher level" and were correctly classified by the children. A general thrust of these studies seems to coincide with Rosenthal's well-known and debated conclusion that pupils' achievement, regardless of ability, will generally be close to the teacher's level of expectation for his pupils. The higher the expectation of the teacher, the higher the achievement of pupils.

An inveterate obstacle to learning is that teachers talk too much. They seem to equate talking with teaching. They seem to think that in order to teach, they have to talk when it may be that, with some teachers, the converse obtains: when they are talking, they are not teaching. No one of us who works with Interaction Analysis will say that the more children talk, the more they will learn, because it depends more on the quality of the talk rather than the quantity of it. We say that when pupils have opportunities to speak, they muster ideas and analyze, synthesize, and evaluate them before they speak. In the speaking process, thoughts are tested, reinforced, and clarified. When a teacher does most or all of the talking, he misses the chance to peek inside the brains of the pupils. When children talk, their ideas can be commended, reinforced, clarified, or extended; some of their thoughts signal the need for reteaching certain content or attitudes.

The two-thirds rule formulated by Flanders and corroborated by other researchers states that two-thirds of the time someone is talking in a classroom, that two-thirds of this time it is the teacher, and that two-thirds of teacher talk is autocratic talk. This finding introduces the enduring problems of classroom climate that teachers produce by the things that come out of their mouths.

The epigram, "Sticks and stones may break your bones, but names will never hurt you," is in the main fallacious. There is not much truth in it. The kinds of spontaneous talk a teacher uses with pupils during social studies lessons either enhances boys' and girls' self-concepts or it deteriorates their self-concepts. What teachers say affects pupils either positively or negatively: pupils feel comfortable and will respond easily, or they feel uncomfortable and will become taciturn. For example, in a discussion of a topic, you might hear these kinds of teacher statements following pupil comments: "It's easy to see you haven't read the textbook or you wouldn't have given an idea like that," or "Your idea is really farfetched," or "If you knew what you were suggesting, you would never take that position," or finally "A few people in the country have the same idea, but they are regarded as uninformed."

The separate studies by Flanders (*24*), Amidon (*1*), and Schantz (*59*) indicated that indirect or democratic verbal patterns of teachers were associated with higher pupil achievement and more desirable attitudes toward their teachers, peers, and work. The work of Hughes (*44*), Perkins (*54*), and Bellack (*6*) corroborate the need for improved classroom climate. My own analysis (*39*) of the verbal behavior of fifth grade social studies teachers highlights the problem: teachers of above average children used more democratic talk than did teachers of below average children. That is putting it kindly. Actually teachers of below average children tended to be autocratic in their general verbal patterns. And the less able children are the very ones who need encouragement, empathy, and clarification of ideas. A poststudy (*40*) showed that children's interests in the social studies correlated highly with the teachers' verbal pattern; pupils of teachers with indirect patterns of talk had higher interest in social studies than did pupils of teachers who used predominantly autocratic talk.

It is evident that teachers can change their verbal behavior through training (*25, 41, 48, 63, 66*). As I work with teachers who desire to improve their talk with children, these are some of the knots that are difficult to saw through:

1. When some teachers talk, they use autocratic talk, i.e., they lecture, direct, and criticize more than they use democratic talk, i.e., than they

accept feelings and ideas, praise, and ask questions. (Of course, both kinds are needed according to the specific instance, but a stronger reliance on democratic talk produces higher pupil achievement.)

2. Some teachers use more democratic talk than is warranted and when autocratic talk is more desirable.

3. Some teachers, never having been told that autocratic talk can be used legitimately with children, experience guilt feelings when they use it. After using autocratic talk with pupils, some teachers have admitted that they try and make it up to the pupil sometime during the rest of the school day.

4. Many teacher's questions are literal and emphasize memory instead of higher mental processes.

5. Some teachers have a tendency to answer their own questions.

6. Pupils' ideas that differ from the teacher's ideas are often either criticized, challenged, given little attention, or ignored.

7. Commendable pupil ideas are sometimes given little or no praise. After praiseworthy pupil talk, the teacher begins to give additional information instead of using praise.

8. Praise is too often general instead of specific. Pupils fail to know what they have done right.

9. Even after training, some teachers have difficulty knowing when to criticize, ask questions, or give information.

10. Pupils are often given little time to think of a response to the teacher's question. There are few extended periods of silence, i.e., ten seconds or longer.

11. On broad topics pupils respond one after the other; but the teacher often fails to react to the responses, and the pupils are unable to tell which responses are correct.

12. A few pupils monopolize the conversation; some teachers fail to bring reticent pupils into the conversation.

One note of caution is needed. Any inservice effort to improve teachers' verbal behavior should be on a voluntary basis; that is, the most effective improvements come when teachers recognize their need and voluntarily enter a training program. Imposed training by supervisors smacks of the same verbal pattern we are trying to change in teachers.

Listening in the Social Studies

The total time spent in speaking activities during the social studies is the identical amount of time in which pupils are engaged in listening. In my investigation cited earlier in the paper, this amount would be about three-quarters of the time for fifth grade pupils. In the junior and senior high school, we would expect that pupils would be listening for even greater proportions of time. Teaching the listening skills seems to be omitted because of the mistaken notion that everybody knows how to listen.

Whenever a teacher gives information, or a pupil recites, or there is teacher-pupil verbal interaction, the rest of the class is usually supposed to be listening. If you observe social studies lessons, you see pupils looking at and examining objects on their desks, looking around the room, drawing, and communicating verbally or nonverbally to neighbors. Only a small fraction of the class seems to be paying attention. Now I would not like to think that pupils resemble me when I tune out speakers in church or at departmental or college faculty meetings. Pupils, however, may be listening even though they give little evidence of it. Of course, just because one appears to be paying attention guarantees little. As mentioned previously, much of the conversation in social studies classrooms is low-level talk based largely on recall of knowledge, so I suspect that only those who read their assignments and have good memories display the most interest in listening. The point to be made is that listening activities need to be interesting if children are to engage in listening.

Another problem arises when pupils do not know what the aims of the lesson are or what they are supposed to be listening for. To preclude desultory conversation, at the outset of the lesson the teacher ought to describe the objectives or purposes of the discussion. Even better, these aims should be written on the chalkboard for easy referral.

We have strong evidence that listening comprehension is equal to or superior to reading comprehension for children at the lower grade levels and for less endowed pupils (*35, 65, 68, 69, 71, 72, 73*). It seems that teachers have not always made use of this finding when faced with children who are reading below grade level. We may suppose that listening skills are used poorly in group situations where so many distractions exist, but we know that listening skills are improved when the pupil is a member of a small group or when he focuses on a television program, a listening station, a tape recorder, or a phonograph record.

Whenever the language arts other than listening are used for instructional purposes, evaluation closely follows the activity. For instance, when a pupil speaks, what he says is appraised for grammar and accuracy of content; when a pupil writes, his paper is examined for accuracy of content and correctness of style and mechanics; and when a pupil reads during seatwork, he is asked to recite or write. But when listening is assigned, an evaluation of the input is rarely even made. Besides, all tests cover the material in the textbook, do they not? Why listen, pupils think, when they can read the textbook a few nights before the test. Except for the few pupils who are highly motivated, listening would probably be significantly improved if some measurement of listening followed closely the activity of listening.

Writing in the Social Studies

A few problems of writing will be discussed briefly. First, we need much more writing in social studies than the two percent found in fifth grade lessons. Nearly any learning placed in a functional setting is better than isolated or contrived learning, and the skills of writing are no exception. Moreover, of all the curriculum areas, the social studies area offers the most opportunities for both practical and personal writing.

The writing that children do is too prescribed. Edmund (23) found that, in a sample of 186 seventh graders, more than half had never had the opportunity or responsibility for choosing their own topic. We have Clark's evidence (11) that children respond best when they write about themselves and their emotional reactions to experiences. If the social studies offer viable, dynamic, and emotional experiences and issues that coincide with what children experience in their lives, the wealth of activities affords a reservoir of writing potentiality of an imaginative and creative nature. Indeed, the motivation offered by such a program would enrich and benefit all of the language arts when used in social studies instructions. The simultaneous benefit to the social studies *per se* would be appreciable.

Summary

The purpose of the paper has been to identify from the research literature some major concerns in the use of the language arts in teaching the social studies. Of all the curriculum areas, the social studies area offers a framework within which the functional use of the skills of the language arts can be taught effectively. Reading and writing require more emphasis during the social studies period. The problems of reading include the readability of textbooks, encyclopedias, and other supplementary materials as well as the vocabulary and conceptual load. These problems require each teacher of the social studies to be a teacher of reading. The low level of talk in classrooms, the overwhelming monopolization of talk by the teacher, and the lack of spontaneous teacher-pupil verbal interaction related to classroom climate characterize pressing needs for change. Listening comprehension is equal to or greater than reading comprehension for many elementary school children, but success in listening on any level of education depends on teaching, listening, motivating pupils to listen, setting purposes for listening, and evaluating the listening activity. The chief problem with respect to writing is simply that considerably more opportunity for writing is needed, and the assignments ought to be based on the emotional reactions of pupils to ideas and issues in the social studies which are a part of their lives.

References

1. Amidon, Edmund, and Ned A. Flanders. "The Effects of Direct and Indirect Teacher Influence on Dependent-Prone Students Learning Geometry," *Journal of Educational Psychology,* 52 (December 1961), 286-291.
2. Arnsdorf, Val E. "Readability of Basal Social Studies Materials," *Reading Teacher,* 16 (January 1963), 243-246.
3. Arnsdorf, Val E. "A Study of Intermediate Grade Children's Understanding of Basal Social Studies Materials," *California Journal of Educational Research,* 14 (March 1963), 67-73.
4. Arnsdorf, Val E. "Time and Space Terms in Basal Social Studies Materials," *California Journal of Educational Research,* 14 (January 1963), 23-29.
5. Arnsdorf, Val E. "An Investigation of the Teaching of Chronology in the Sixth Grade," *Journal of Experimental Education,* 29 (March 1961), 307-313.
6. Bellack, Arno A., et al. *The Language of the Classroom,* New York: Teachers College, Columbia University, United States Office of Education Cooperative Research Project No. 1497, 1963. Arno A. Bellack, et al. *The Language of the Classroom,* Part Two. New York: Institute of Psychological Research, Teachers College, Columbia University, United States Office of Education Cooperative Research Project No. 2023, 1965.
7. Betts, Emmett A. *Foundations of Reading Instruction.* New York: American Book Company, 1946, Chapter 22.
8. Carmichael, Dennis R. "Developing Map Reading Skills and Geographic Understanding by Means of Conceptual Teaching Methods," doctoral thesis, University of California at Berkeley, 1965. *Dissertation Abstracts,* 26 (June 1966), 7176.
9. Carner, R. L., and W. D. Sheldon. "Problems in the Development of Concepts Through Reading," *Elementary School Journal,* 55 (December 1954), 226-229.
10. Chase, W. Linwood, and Gilbert M. Wilson. "Preference Studies in Elementary School Social Studies," *Journal of Education,* 140 (April 1958), 1-28.
11. Clark, Gwyn R. "Writing Situations to Which Children Respond," *Elementary English,* 31 (March 1954), 150-155.
12. Clegg, A. A., G. T. Farley, and R. J. Curran. "Analyzing the Cognitive Level of Classroom Questions: A Preliminary Report," paper read at the Fourth Conference on Instruction, University of Massachusetts, May 8, 1967.
13. Clegg, A. A., G. T. Farley, and R. J. Curran. "Training Teachers to Analyze the Cognitive Level of Classroom Questioning," Research Report No. 1, Applied Research Training Program, School of Education, University of Massachusetts, June 1967.
14. Clegg, Ambrose A., Jr., Alberta P. Sebolt, and Paul Benoit. "Can Children Learn to Raise the Cognitive Level of Their Own Thinking?" Research Report No. 4, School of Education, University of Massachusetts, November 1967.
15. Crabtree, Charlotte. "Inquiry Approaches to Learning Concepts and Generalizations in Social Studies," *Social Education,* 30 (October 1966), 407-411, 414.

16. Curry, Robert L. "Subject Preferences of 1,111 Fifth Graders," *Peabody Journal of Education*, 41 (July 1963), 23-37.

17. Davis, O. L., Jr. "Children Can Learn Complex Concepts," *Educational Leadership*, 17 (December 1959), 170-175.

18. Davis, O. L., Jr. "Cognitive Objectives Revealed by Classroom Questions Asked by Social Studies Student-Teachers," *Peabody Journal of Education*, 45 (July 1967), 21-26.

19. Duffey, Robert V. "Helping the Less-Able Reader," *Social Education*, 25 (April 1961), 182-184.

20. Duffey, Robert V. "Elementary School Teachers' Reading," unpublished manuscript, 1967.

21. Durrell, Donald D., and Leonard J. Savignano. "Classroom Enrichment Through Pupil Specialties," *Journal of Education*, 138 (February 1956), 1-31.

22. Edgerton, Ronald B. "How Difficult Are Children's Encyclopedias? A Second Report," *Elementary School Journal*, 55 (December 1954), 219-225.

23. "Educational News and Editorial Comment," *Elementary School Journal*, 58 (December 1957), 129.

24. Flanders, Ned A. *Teacher Influence, Pupil Attitudes, and Achievement.* Ann Arbor: University of Michigan, United States Office of Education, Cooperative Research Project No. 297, 1962.

25. Flanders, Ned A., et al. *Helping Teachers Change Their Behavior.* Ann Arbor: University of Michigan, United States Office of Education, N.D.E.A., Project Numbers 1721012 and 7-32-0560-171, April 1963.

26. Floyd, William D. "An Analysis of the Oral Questioning Activity in Selected Colorado Primary Classrooms," doctoral thesis, Colorado State College, 1960.

27. Foley, Harriet M. "Preferences of Sixth Grade Children for Certain Social Studies Activities," unpublished master's thesis, Boston University, 1951.

28. Francis, James F. "Preferences and Readability of Paperback Books," *Journal of Education*, 146 (April 1964), 16-18.

29. Francis, James F., and Mabel S. Noall. "Reading Patterns to Meet Environmental Demands—Vocational Guidance Through Paperbacks," paper presented to the American Personnel and Guidance Association Convention, Denver, March 29, 1961.

30. Gates, Arthur I. "The Teaching of Reading—Objective Evidence Versus Opinion," *Phi Delta Kappan*, 43 (February 1962), 197-205.

31. Gill, Clark. "Interpretations of Indefinite Expressions of Time," *Social Education*, 26 (December 1962), 454-456.

32. Goebel, George. "Reactions of Selected Sixth Grade Pupils to Social Studies Learning Activities Chosen by Their Teachers in the Public Schools of Topeka, Kansas," doctoral thesis, University of Kansas, 1965. *Dissertation Abstracts*, 26 (January 1966), 3755-3756.

33. Gray, W. S. "Theme of the Conference," *Improving Reading in Content Fields*, Supplementary Educational Monograph, No. 62. Chicago: University of Chicago Press, January 1947, 4-5.

34. Haffner, Hyman. "A Study of Vocabulary Load and Social Concept Burden of Fifth and Sixth Grade Social Studies, History, and Geography Text-

books," doctoral thesis, University of Pittsburgh, 1959. *Dissertation Abstracts,* 20 (May 1960), 4311-4312.

35. Hampleman, R. S. "Comparison of Listening and Reading Comprehension Ability of Fourth and Sixth Grade Pupils," *Elementary English,* 35 (January 1958), 49-53.

36. Herber, Harold L. "An Experiment in Teaching Reading Through Social Studies Context," in J. Allen Figurel (Ed.), *Changing Concepts of Reading Instruction.* Proceedings of the International Reading Association, 6, 1961, 122-124.

37. Herman, Wayne L., Jr. "How Intermediate Children Rank the Subjects," *Journal of Educational Research,* 56 (April 1963), 435-436.

38. Herman, Wayne L., Jr. "The Use of Language Arts in Social Studies Lessons," *American Educational Research Journal,* 4 (March 1967), 117-124.

39. Herman, Wayne L., Jr. "An Analysis of the Activities and Verbal Behavior of Selected Fifth Grade Social Studies Classes," *Journal of Educational Research,* 60 (April 1967), 339-345.

40. Herman, Wayne L., Jr. "The Relationship Between Teachers' Verbal Behavior and Children's Interests in the Social Studies," *Peabody Journal of Education,* 43 (November 1965), 157-160.

41. Herman, Wayne L., Jr., and Robert V. Duffey. "Study of the Efficacy of a Training Program in Interaction Analysis for Elementary and Secondary School Teachers," unpublished manuscript, 1968.

42. Hill, Walter. "Content Textbook: Help or Hindrance," *Journal of Reading,* 10 (March 1967), 408-413.

43. Holmes, Ethel E. "School Subjects Preferred by Children," *Appraising the Elementary-School Program,* Sixteenth Yearbook of the National Elementary Principal. Washington, D. C.: National Educational Association, 1937, 336-344.

44. Hughes, Marie M., et al. *The Assessment of the Quality of Teaching: A Research Report.* Salt Lake City: University of Utah, United States Office of Education Cooperative Research Project No. 353, 1959.

45. Hunkins, Francis P. "The Influence of Analysis and Evaluation Questions on Achievement in Sixth Grade Social Studies," *Educational Leadership Research,* Supplement 1 (January 1968), 326-332.

46. Jarolimek, John, and Clifford D. Foster. "Quantitative Concepts in Fifth Grade Social Studies Textbooks," *Elementary School Journal,* 59 (May 1959), 437-442.

47. Jersild, Arthur T., and Ruth J. Tasch. *Children's Interests and What They Suggest for Education.* New York: Bureau of Publications, Teachers College, Columbia University, 1949, 28, 146.

48. Kirk, Jeffrey. "Effects of Teaching the Minnesota System of Interaction Analysis to Intermediate Grade Student Teachers," doctoral thesis, Temple University, 1964. *Dissertation Abstracts,* 25 (August 1964), 1031.

49. Liske, Wilfred W. "An Investigation of the Readability of Selected Juvenile Encyclopedia Material by the Cloze Procedure and a Comparison of Results with Readability Formulas," doctoral thesis, University of Maryland, 1968.

50. Lyda, W. J., and Verna A. Robinson. "Quantitative Concepts in Selected Social Studies Textbooks for Second Grade," *Elementary School Journal,* 65 (December 1964), 159-162.

51. Maynard, Glenn. "Value of Twenty-five Cent Books for Independent Recreational Reading," *Peabody Journal of Education,* 41 (September 1963), 86-90.

52. Mills, Robert E., and Jean R. Richardson. "What Do Publishers Mean by Grade Level?" *Reading Teacher,* 16 (March 1963), 359-362.

53. Penty, Ruth. *Reading Ability and High School Dropouts.* 19-30. New York: Bureau of Publications, Teachers College, Columbia University, 1956.

54. Perkins, Hugh. "Classroom Behavior and Underachievement," *American Educational Research Journal,* 2 (January 1965), 1-12.

55. Preston, Ralph C. *Teaching Social Studies in the Elementary School* (3rd ed.). New York: Holt, Rinehart and Winston, 1968, 241-242.

56. Rice, Joseph P. "A Comparative Study of Academic Interest Patterns Among Selected Groups of Exceptional and Normal Intermediate Children," *California Journal of Educational Research,* 14 (May 1963), 131-137.

57. Robinson, H. Alan. "Reading Skills Employed in Solving Social Studies Problems," *Reading Teacher,* 18 (January 1965), 263-269.

58. Russell, David, and Ibrahim Q. Saadeh. "Qualitative Levels in Children's Vocabularies," *Journal of Educational Psychology,* 53 (August 1962), 170-174.

59. Schantz, Betty. "An Experimental Study Comparing the Effects of Verbal Recall by Children in Direct and Indirect Teaching Methods as a Tool of Measurement," doctoral thesis, Pennsylvania State University, 1963. *Dissertation Abstracts,* 25 (August 1964), 1054.

60. Smith, Charlene W. "The Vocabulary of Factual Reading Materials," *Educational Forum,* 27 (May 1963), 443-447.

61. Smith, H. P., and E. U. Dechant. *Psychology in Teaching Reading.* Englewood Cliffs, New Jersey: Prentice Hall, 1961, 245.

62. Stewart, Dorothy H. "Children's Preferences in Types of Assignment," unpublished master's thesis, Boston University, 1945.

63. Storlie, Theodore R. "Selected Characteristics of Teachers Whose Verbal Behavior is Influenced by an Inservice Course in Interaction Analysis," doctoral thesis, University of Minnesota, 1961. *Dissertation Abstracts,* 22 (May 1962), 3941.

64. Taba, Hilda, Samuel Levine, and Freeman F. Elzey. *Thinking in Elementary Children.* San Francisco: San Francisco State College, United States Office of Education, Cooperative Research Project No. 1574, April 1964.

65. Triggs, Francis O. "A Comparison of Auditory and Silent Presentations of Reading Comprehension Tests," *The Fourteenth Yearbook, National Council on Measurements Used in Education.* Princeton, New Jersey: Educational Testing Service, 1957, 1-7.

66. Waimon, Morton, D. "Feedback in Classrooms: A Study of Corrective Teaching Responses," *Journal of Experimental Education,* 30 (June 1962), 355-359.

67. Washburne, J. N. "The Use of Questions in Social Science Material," *Journal of Educational Psychology,* 20 (May 1929), 321-359.

68. Webb, W. B., and E. J. Wallon. "Comprehension by Reading versus Hearing," *Journal of Applied Psychology,* 40 (August 1956), 237-240.

69. Westover, F. L. "A Comparison of Listening and Reading as a Means of Testing," *Journal of Educational Research,* 52 (September 1958), 23-26.

70. Witt, Mary. "A Study of the Effectiveness of Certain Techniques of Reading Instruction in Developing the Ability of Junior High Students to Conceptualize Social Studies Content," *Journal of Educational Research,* 56 (December 1962), 198-204.

71. Witty, P. and R. A. Sizemore. "Studies in Listening, I. Relative Values of Oral and Visual Presentations," *Elementary English,* 36 (January 1959), 1958), 538-552.

72. Witty, P., and R. A. Sizemore. "Studies in Listening, II. Relative Values of Oral and Visual Presentations," *Elementary English,* 36 (January 1959), 59-70.

73. Witty, P., and R. A. Sizemore. "Studies in Listening, III. The Effectiveness of Visual and Auditory Presentations with Changes in Ages and Grade Levels," *Elementary English,* 36 (February 1959), 130-140.

Newer Approaches to Handling
the Vocabulary Problem

RALPH C. PRESTON
University of Pennsylvania

THIS PAPER is chiefly concerned with problems arising from the pupil's encounter with words in his reading which are not in his meaning vocabulary. His meaning vocabulary consists of those words whose meanings he recognizes when he hears or reads them.

I realize that to some teachers *the* vocabulary problem resides in teaching word attack skills. To be sure, in the primary grades, deficient reading comprehension is usually due to lack of facility in decoding words, whether their meanings are known or not. This condition also applies to some individuals in advanced grades. For such individuals, the extent to which lagging reading comprehension is due to meager meaning vocabulary can be ascertained only after we eliminate poor word attack skills, distractibility, and perceptual difficulties as interfering factors.

The fact remains that, beginning in fourth grade, most pupils can decode almost any word. Words that are troublesome for them are those whose meanings (or at least certain of their meanings) are unknown or are only vaguely known. Even first grade pupils who are struggling with decoding should be assisted simultaneously by their teachers to extend and enrich knowledge of word meanings.

A second fact of importance is that the long standing complaint of teachers that social studies books are too difficult stems from the books' bombardment of the pupil with large numbers of strange words or familiar words with technical meanings (such as the word "common" in the term "common law"). Teachers assert that as a consequence of this state of affairs, pupils typically bewail reading assignments even if only of moderate length, that pupils passively glean a few random facts and ideas from them, that pupils frequently misinterpret the author's point, and that they skip some passages altogether.

There is thus ample justification for dealing here with the problem of enlarging meaning vocabulary rather than with the popular problem of teaching school beginners and retarded readers how speech is represented by written symbols and how to crack the code. That is not the job of

21

social studies instruction. I shall have my hands full in concentrating upon the more difficult problem of teaching word meanings.

Traditional Practices

Most teachers are aware that vocabulary is a chief stumbling block to better comprehension of published social studies materials. Consequently, teachers have tried to improve the situation by teaching vocabulary directly. At the elementary school level, they tend to teach word meanings as part of the directed reading lesson, familiarizing pupils with the meaning of new words which will be encountered in the reading of the ensuing social studies lesson. Teachers' guides accompanying social studies textbooks for elementary schools are likely to be helpful here in supplying a list of the new words which the pupil is about to encounter and with suggestions of how to discuss the words with the class.

In secondary schools, some teachers follow a similar procedure or make up word lists of their own after the fashion of Cole's once widely used *Teachers' Handbook of Technical Vocabulary* (7). It is more common at the secondary school level, however, for teachers to assign a textbook chapter without preparing students for the semantic rigors it may possess. Yet it is disastrous for the learning of some students thus to ignore the vocabulary problem. I can illustrate this from an investigation (17) I conducted of the knowledge possessed by 79 eleventh grade students concerning ten key words in their American history textbook. The average intelligence level was above average, a fact which led the teachers to believe the students did not need to work on vocabulary. As a part of the investigation, students were instructed to write out their definitions or explanations of each term. How well did they do? They defined or explained an average of only three of the ten words with reasonable accuracy. By way of illustrating their faulty knowledge of the words, I cite one student's explanation of *"arbitration"* as "cheating against the government" and another student's definition of "moratorium" as "a place of death, such as a funeral parlor." I submit that most students have trouble with the technical vocabulary of social studies.

Leads from Linguistics

My point of departure in this paper is the proposition that the traditional direct teaching of vocabulary, whether through the directed reading lesson or through having pupils master word definitions is, when used alone, inadequate. I did not always think so (18). I had been overly impressed by research studies showing that direct teaching could promote a pupil's reading comprehension of a given passage or chapter. But if we think in terms of genuinely and permanently expanding a pupil's vocabulary as a part of his continuous growth, I doubt if any teacher is satisfied with the results. As far as isolated drill goes, Horn (*11*) brought out a generation ago that it is of small avail. Attempts to separate the vocabulary problem from other aspects of reading social studies materials will, I fear, continue to prove disappointing.

Today we have leads from the field of linguistics for the teaching of vocabulary that promise to be more productive than direct teaching of word meanings. Superficially, its implied approaches may appear old, not new. When we are reassured by linguists of how writing and oral reading, for example, can build resourcefulness in dealing with the vocabulary aspect of reading comprehension, we are, to be sure, using old and well-known devices. But we are using them in new ways and for new purposes, and we are investing the pupil with new power.

The impact of linguistics upon the teaching of reading and grammar in recent years has had a shattering effect (*4, 5, 6*). Its implications for fields in which reading plays an important role, such as social studies, are unmistakable but as yet only furtively explored. In any case, when we teach social studies today, we are forced to think of the structure of the language we employ as we are already accustomed to think about the concepts we wish to transmit or which we wish our pupils to discover. The linguists have buttressed the understanding of the process whereby the all-important social studies concept is either illuminated or dulled by the manner in which it is expressed. We now know that in the conveying of ideas, vocabulary is an element of language closely intertwined with other elements and not easily pulled apart from them.

From the broad acreage of linguistics with its many resources for possible fruitful exploitation by teachers, I shall take up in this paper two areas, intonation and semantics.

Implications of the Study of Intonation

One of the clearest applications of linguistics to teaching vocabulary is its findings with respect to intonational patterns (*4*). Intonation is the melody of speech, the rise and fall of the voice, its emphases, its pauses, its rhythm. Knowledge of intonational phenomena is of the utmost importance in reading. One linguist (*13*) expressed it thus: ". . . the ability to relate the melody of speech to the written page is the key to good reading. Good readers do it; poor readers don't."

All children should learn that intonational patterns, obviously basic to meaning in a conversational setting, are only crudely revealed in writing. Writing perforce not only neglects intonation, it also neglects gestures, significant glances, and similar conveyers of meaning. It is partly because a written sentence conceals intonation and other features accompanying oral speech that many written sentences are not easy to understand. The hearer of a *spoken* sentence catches the intonational signals that reveal the sentence structure. The child, long before he enters school, learns to detect such signals. Many *written* sentences, on the other hand, can be read in more than one way. For this reason, when the reader is not fully entered into the context of what he is reading, when he is not in harmony with the mood of the author (a not uncommon condition of any of us at certain times), he is badly handicapped. Alternative intonations not intended by the author carry other connotations.

Sometimes even subtle intonational differences are significant for meaning. Consider the sentence: "It is not the business of insurance to prevent loss." The author intended the stress to be upon "prevent loss." One pupil who knew the meaning of every one of the words, placed stress on the word "loss" and so reacted to the sentence by thinking: "Then what *is* it that insurance prevents?" He was off on the wrong track, since it was not the author's intent to answer that question at all. The point of the author was that insurance does not prevent anything, least of all loss; rather, insurance *minimizes risk*. But writing does not transmit voice tone, so such errors occur. Another pupil might quite as conceivably have stressed in that sentence the word "business." He might have thought: "Apparently insurance prevents loss, all right, but that is not the insurance companies' business; it is merely an automatic spin-off of the business that happens to benefit the clients." Such pitfalls in comprehension exist in scores of critical sentences in any book.

Normally, the well-motivated, intelligent reader will quickly detect the implausibility of his interpretation of the intonation of a sentence, whereupon he will almost immediately correct himself, often unconsciously and without even needing to give the misread sentence a second look. One must remember, however, that schools contain many pupils who are only moderately motivated and only modestly endowed with intelligence. The main reason for teaching about the relationship between intonation and written communication is to reduce one prominent element of frustration in reading, thereby increasing motivation and effective intelligence.

It is probably obvious that we do not need always to reconstruct written messages into oral messages. Much writing has its own dialect which actually sounds awkward when spoken or read aloud. Some fourth graders can comprehend easily and directly such written dialect, although most individuals probably do not exercise the skill with facility until the high school years.

All reading calls for alert readers who are continually seeking to come to terms with the author. If the pupil in the example had not known the meaning of the word "insurance," he would have been, of course, in still deeper water; but teaching him the meaning of "insurance" would not totally have solved the meaning problem for him. We can and should teach children from the very start of their formal education that certain written material is a poor substitute for person-to-person confrontation and communication and that even good readers should resort to oral reconstruction in the reading of *any* written material when a passage begins to lose sense.

Given the foregoing information, what approaches might be adopted? A few suggestions follow.

Oral reading of dictated records. In kindergarten and first grade the teacher should record on the chalkboard pupil speech about social studies. This is a desirable daily practice even before children can read. The procedure drives home the primacy of speech in language and illustrates visibly to the pupils that this writing is nothing more nor less than a record of speech, and a rather crude record. The product may be reminiscent of the well-known reading chart used in the teaching of reading, but one should not be deceived by its similarity. It is a summary record of a *social studies* lesson, or part of a lesson, as spoken by members of the class, in which new and technical vocabulary is included and a record of which is constructed by the teacher. The transcription is there to be read again and again (by the teacher if the children cannot read them). Normally, each sentence is read first by the pupil who spoke it. Others, using the natural intonation in which it was originally spoken, may repeat it. The poverty of the written record becomes apparent when it is read by a pupil who had not been present when the lesson was held or recorded. Later, when the class receives social studies textbooks, pupils will discover that each page is a similar record of a social studies lesson, this time printed in book form and formulated by some unknown person called the author.

Word analysis is a necessary part of the instruction at this level. Nevertheless, the *emphasis* should be placed upon reading an entire sentence in order to avoid the expressionless, word-by-word pattern of reading in which each word receives approximately equal stress.

Oral reading from books. Oral reading should be continued in every grade of school but not in the traditional way of pupils' taking turns in reading successive sections of a chapter. Rather, the teacher should restrict oral reading to selected sections from the book which contain exceptionally important ideas and key technical terms. The pupil to do the reading should first have read the passage silently so that he has become sufficiently familiar with its ideas and the structure of each of its sentences so that his intonation will resemble the transmission of the material in normal speech. Such reading provides further opportunity for pupils to *use* and to *hear* unfamiliar words in context. For a pupil just to *say* an unfamiliar word, just to let it glide off his tongue, is an educational event of high magnitude. Aside from its being fun for him, the mastery of its pronunciation and its meaning gives him an improved self-image—the product of his pride and power in acquiring a new word. It becomes a new tool, a new avenue to knowledge. It should be unnecessary to add that no child should be asked to read orally if the book is not at his instructional level. Failure to perform adequately before an audience of his peers is a humiliating experience which can destroy self-acceptance and impair future learning.

Writing.   Another implication of linguistics is the desirability of having pupils manipulate words through writing. Writing is a neglected activity in social studies teaching. Herman (*10*) found that less than two percent of social studies lessons was spent in writing. Once pupils reach the stage of fluency in writing (some as young as eight are enthusiastic and productive writers), writing should be frequent. Teachers can at least have their pupils keep personal logs in which to record their daily social studies learning. Numerous opportunities exist for writing (*16*). Having the pupil create his own formulation of social studies content gives still additional use of the burgeoning vocabulary of the social studies.

Dramatization.   Another lesson to be inferred from linguistics is the value of dramatization and role-playing in connection with episodes drawn from the social studies. Here again pupils can *use* and *hear* the vocabulary in live context. Five- or ten-minute dramatizations of episodes once or twice a week can be quite informal and unrehearsed. The awkwardness occurring when a group is unaccustomed to informal dramatization soon wears off, and its contribution to social studies learning becomes evident to pupils and teacher alike.

Implications of Semantics

The field of semantics, held at arm's length by some linguists as an unwanted stepchild, also makes important contributions to vocabulary teaching. Semantics, concerned with the meaning of words, advances the important axiom that a person does not get or extract meaning *from* a word; he can only give meaning *to* a word. And he can give it meaning only in terms of his own experience, either real or vicarious. The meaning a child gives to the term "national forest," for example, depends on his experience with forests and with what is implied by nationalization. With respect to the concrete concept of "forest," he may have seen a picture of one taken from the air and he may have read or heard forest stories such as Hansel and Gretel. But does he understand the vastness of the forest and its relative darkness and coolness on a hot summer's day? What does he know about its wild life? Pupil A visited a national forest, became acquainted with a forest ranger, learned from the ranger about the causes and dangers of forest fires, responded emotionally to the majesty there, went swimming in its lakes, used its camping facilities, and saw a few deer. He is able to attach greater meaning to the term "national forest" than Pupil B whose only comparable experience is a walk in a patch of woods, perhaps littered by picnickers and damaged by axes and knives.

Experiences with underlying concepts. The social studies are inherently difficult because so many terms relate to concepts that remain outside the experience and interest of pupils and are quite abstract, such as "liberty," "incorporation," and "enforcement." Such terms stand for conditions or processes which cannot be observed or tested. Hence, teachers are obliged to supply verbal descriptions, illustrations, stories in which the concept operates, and other expedients in an effort to fill sufficiently the gaps in their pupils' background so that the reading of the words will take on some color and depth of meaning.

In other words, concepts often have to be taught before a word is understood. Pupils who have difficulty in learning about latitude and longitude will not necessarily be helped at all by being told the definitions of those terms. Such pupils may first need to learn how to locate a particular cell in a grid. A grid-like arrangement—perhaps a classroom whose seats are set in rows—needs to be observed. Pupils can learn to locate a particular cell of a grid by naming the two coordinate numbers which denote the horizontal and perpendicular rows, respectively. For example, Johnny sits in row 4, seat 3: When pupils turn to the grid of a map or a globe, the problem shifts. They now can no longer be satisfied with locating a cell, but they must describe the location of a *point*—perhaps the location of an air crash or a lonely island. They are now working with geographic coordinates and are helped by the concept of "ordered pairs of numbers" as taught these days in the new math. Until these various stages of concepts dealing with grids are understood, the terms latitude and longitude will remain obscure.

At the high school level, too, a vocabulary problem may be difficult unless the concept problem is first tackled. In a high school course which contained a unit on sociology, the term "reference group" was introduced to the class. The teacher explained that the term designates a group or a social category whose norms one adopts or accepts. The term itself was new to the students, but the real barrier to their understanding was two conceptual shortcomings (which were later overcome through sharing of personal observations and experiences: (a) students had difficulty in perceiving society as divided into distinct and conglomerate groups. How, some of them asked, can a reference group be a family, a friendship, the employees in an office, the citizens of a nation, and one's classmates? (b) There was also difficulty in their grasping the concept of "being influenced." After all, it takes a degree of mature introspection to realize that one is being led to view favorably (or unfavorably) certain ideas and ways of living by one's family or by a clique or by a teacher. Probably all teachers have had pupils who thought that their view of things was the only view and who were surprised at the idea that they had been influenced or "taken in" by forces in their milieu. The writer has taught adults who were aghast when it was suggested to them that they may have been *conditioned* to think that Christians were morally superior to non-Christians.

Identifying terms with dated meanings.   Semanticists also draw attention to words which were coined to describe processes which were once useful but which are now no longer appropriate because of changes in society which demand new viewpoints and new solutions. One such term is "national sovereignty." Some linguists (*14*) and some social scientists, Toynbee (*19*), for example, believe that continued use of that term blocks the development of international law that might prevent world disaster. But the old term is clung to. It has a noble ring to the ears of some people and is used as though the words were arguments in themselves. There is some reason for believing that continued repetition of Bismarck's statement that "Politics is the doctrine of the possible" keeps alive a cliché that is used by politicians today to gloss over unsavory compromise and corruption and to thwart idealistic constituents. By way of another example, an economist (*9*) writes in *Newsweek* that continued obeisance to the term "gold standard" confuses leaders in a period when gold no longer determines the quality of money. The semantically oriented teacher has his pupils stop, look, listen, and, above all, analyze the origin and present use of such terms.

Identifying terms used in blurred context.   Semanticists call attention to blurring or stereotyping. One blurring phenomenon occurs when class names (such as "police," "John Birchers," "professors," etc.) are used in a way which obliterates distinctions among the members of the class. A newspaper editorial denounces hippies and yippies, all of whom, it avers, are parasites and nihilists. Generalizations are made about the attitudes of the Negro community, women drivers, the press, today's parents, and so forth. Blurring is not confined to pejorative references. Henry Adams (*1*), in his history, quoted a French visitor to the United States in 1797 who wrote that ". . . it would be no exaggeration to say, in the numerous assemblies of Philadelphia it is impossible to meet with what is called a plain woman." It is not hard to find other examples of sweeping extravagant praise in biographies, obituaries, eulogies, and other such writing.

Another kind of blurring is the practice of identifying a single cause for a complex event. There are pupils who come to school with the idea that prices are high because of the "middle man," that the activities of Wall Street cause both depressions and inflation, and the like. Any oversimplification is a form of blurring. The geographer Augelli (3) has protested two tendencies of teachers and textbooks in their descriptions of Latin America: (a) their lumping of Latin-American cultures as though they were homogeneous, and (b) their assertions that certain unprepossessing features of Latin America's physical environment are an obstacle to the settlement and development of its empty lands. In almost any type of social studies material, pupils should be encouraged to be on the lookout for examples of blurring.

Acquiring sensitivity to careless use of terms. When the semanticists's work has more thoroughly penetrated teacher-training institutions, teachers will spend more time than they presently do in focusing class attention upon careless use of words. Teachers will be more distrustful of relying on definitions of complex terms as keys to understanding, and they will take greater care to teach the concepts which the terms denote and connote. Teachers will have their pupils explore significant words in their books, and spot those words that are not contemporaneously appropriate and those that blur. Pupils will be asked to find examples of these and other semantic lapses in the daily press, in magazines, in their textbooks, and in their supplementary social studies reading of biographies, historical novels, editorials, and reference books. Pupils will be encouraged to write up such incidents as exhibits to be discussed or to be posted on the bulletin board. The semantic approach to social studies content already has been tried out and promises to become a highly productive means of stimulating judicious, critical appraisal of the printed word (15).

Direct Teaching of Vocabulary

Earlier in this paper I questioned the value of direct teaching of vocabulary and noted its relatively low-grade productivity. I conceded, however, that if the direct teaching were used as a *supplement* to a linguistics-oriented approach, it has a modest role to play and deserves a place in the teacher's repertoire.

Two books deserve careful study by every teacher. Deighton's *Vocabulary Development in the Classroom* (8) is probably as sound as any of the myriad books on the subject. Deighton suggests several ways of teaching pupils in any grade how to deal with puzzling words and contexts. One of these ways is to teach the meaning of affixes in the traditional way, but to teach only those which have restricted meanings. Deighton points out the mistake of teaching that *all* common affixes have single meanings. He indicates that most of them have several meanings. For example, the prefix "de-" is often taught as meaning "of" or "from." In reality, it may also denote "down" as in "decline", it may also mean "separation" as in "deprive," etc. Deighton also lists commonly used affixes with *single* variant meanings which are worth teaching, such as the prefix "circum-" meaning "around" and the suffix "-chrome" meaning "colored." Deighton stresses the teaching of pupils how to use English base-words in attacking the meanings of unfamiliar words. The base-word is a familiar English word which also serves as a common denominator for other words. Thus, "press" is a base-word which can be used to give the meanings of the words "compress" and "depression"; "depend" is a base-word which can be used to give meaning to "dependent" and "dependable."

Another useful guide to the direct teaching of vocabulary is Adler's classic, *How to Read a Book* (2). Adler's main point concerning vocabulary is for the reader to learn to spot the really important words in a book. This task can be done, he explains, by learning to detect the author's clues. Some clues are obvious, such as a word placed within quotation marks or a word set in italics. He advises the reader to be on the lookout for occasions when the author quarrels with others about a word, for such a word is always important for that author and in that book. Such a quarrel which neatly illustrates Adler's point appears in one of James' geographies (*12*). In that book, James and his coauthor, Davis, become irate about the use by teachers (and by Aristotle!) of such expressions as "temperate zone" and "torrid zone." " 'Temperate' means 'moderate' or 'not extreme'. . . . In it are the places that hold the world's records for extremes of temperature. . . . It is incorrect and misleading to speak of the 'temperate zone.' When we want to refer to the parts of the world . . . which are regions between 30° and 60° in the Northern and Southern hemispheres . . ." we should speak of the "middle latitudes." It is clear to see from this indignant passage that the authors think "middle latitudes" is a pretty important term!

Broadening the Vocabulary of Nonreaders and Disabled Readers

Thus far I have been speaking about the vocabulary problem as it presents itself among pupils who *can* and who *do* read. What about pupils in the primary grades who have not yet learned to read? What about older pupils who are retarded in their acquisition of reading skills and whose textbooks are at their frustration level—that is, at a difficulty level that causes them to skip many words and to hesitate over other words?

First, consider kindergarten and first grade classes. Few pupils in those grades are independent readers. The problem is obviously and simply solved. If the pupils cannot read the textbook, the teacher can read it to the class, with each pupil following along in his copy of the book and noting at least the illustrations. Accompanied by the teacher's reading, the illustrations are normally sufficiently vivid to help transmit new concepts, to help clarify concepts, and to provide a basis for discussion and exploration. The teacher should avoid turning a social studies class into a word-attack session. The purpose of a social studies lesson is for the pupils to achieve an understanding of selected social concepts. One first grade teacher in a disadvantaged urban area recently told me that she and her class enjoy the experience of having her read the entire social studies textbook to the class, lesson by lesson. Each reading is followed by a searching and productive discussion. At the end of the school year her class was able to construct an interesting and concept-laden scrapbook of pictures, captions, and brief text in which the pupils recorded their reactions to the social studies content and their own extensions of it. The teacher reported that the growth of the pupils' understanding and their control over the vocabulary were substantial.

With older pupils, it is often advisable to postpone the reading of a section until the pupils are thoroughly prepared for it. This work may take several days. The concepts and technical terms of the section can be presented and discussed. The teacher may choose to present the content orally himself. The pupils may then look at their books to discover the way the content is organized there. The headings, pictures, and captions may be explored jointly. The teacher might then ask: "What will we learn from this section? In what order will the topics be studied?" In answering these questions, the pupils will be formulating the structure of the section. The class will eventually be ready for a systematic reading of it. The suggestions given earlier for indirect teaching of vocabulary will fall easily into place.

Even quite poor readers can learn to read at least the table of contents in the textbook. In this way they can master the organization of the units and chapters and learn how the various sections of the book relate. In the process they will learn many important technical terms. In like manner, they can learn to read the captions of pictures, charts, tables, and maps. Vocabulary growth is promoted in the process.

It always pays to see if there is supplementary material on the unit for the less able reader. Librarians can be of great help here. Even if the easier book is not strictly parallel to the textbook organization, it may provide an opportunity to the retarded reader of acquiring social studies content through a successful reading experience.

Finally, "team learning" procedures should be employed. I have demonstrated "team learning" countless times, have observed it demonstrated, and can attest to its success. The class is divided into teams of about three pupils each. Each team includes one good reader who serves as the team captain. Each pupil is given a study guide (a teacher-prepared list of questions covering that day's lesson). Each team captain reads the lesson aloud to his team and then he reads the questions aloud. The pupils recall the answer or may need to look for the answers in their textbooks. When in doubt, members of a team may discuss the question together. Then they consult an answer sheet. The other questions are read, answered, and checked similarly. The scheme assures success and security for the pupil because it enables him to understand what the passage is all about and to check the accuracy of his knowledge immediately. Every child becomes acquainted with the vocabulary of the lesson and responds to every question. He is thus prepared for whatever discussions or tests the teacher may have planned.

Summary

I have attempted to show in this paper that the knowledge of social studies vocabulary of typical pupils is vague and inaccurate and that the direct teaching of vocabulary, when relied upon alone, has proved disappointing. Data and insights from the field of linguistics were presented which suggest that oral reading, writing, and dramatization, if closely tied to the pupil's reading, will enable him consciously to supply elements of spoken language in his reading which are missing in the printed sentence. The contention was made that semantics, a branch of linguistics, provides leads to teachers of how to enrich a pupil's vocabulary by enlarging his experiences and concepts and by helping him analyze words in a way that will advance his critical reading. Certain procedures for the direct teaching of vocabulary were described which may prove effective if used as an accompaniment to the linguistically derived approaches. Finally, means were suggested for stimulating the vocabulary development of pupils whose reading ability is at a low point.

This paper has taken for granted and has avoided laboring the point of the cruciality of the pupil's meaning vocabulary for precise and lucid reading comprehension. Robert Louis Stevenson wrote that "Language is but a poor bull's-eye lantern wherewith to show off the vast cathedral of the world." Language is also the *only* lantern we have for communicating with one another about the cathedral. That's what makes vocabulary in social studies so important.

References

1. Adams, Henry. *The United States in 1800*. Ithaca, New York: Cornell University Press, 1955, 84.
2. Adler, Mortimer J. *How to Read a Book*. New York: Simon and Schuster, 1940, Chapter 10.
3. Augelli, John P. "The Controversial Image of Latin America: A Geographer's View," *Journal of Geography*, 62 (March 1963), 103-116.
4. Botel, Morton. "What Linguistics Says to This Teacher of Reading and Spelling," *Reading Teacher*, 18 (December 1964), 188-193.
5. Carroll, John B. *The Study of Language*, Cambridge, Massachusetts: Harvard University Press, 1963, Chapter 6.
6. Chall, Jeanne S. *Learning to Read: The Great Debate*. New York: McGraw-Hill, 1967.
7. Cole, Luella. *Teacher's Handbook of Technical Vocabulary*. Bloomington, Illinois: Public School Publishing, 1940.
8. Deighton, Lee C. *Vocabulary Development in the Classroom*. New York: Bureau of Publications, Teachers College, Columbia University, 1959.
9. Friedman, Milton. "A Dollar Is a Dollar," *Newsweek*, 69 (May 15, 1967), 58.
10. Herman, Wayne L., Jr. "The Use of Language Arts in Social Studies Lessons," *American Educational Research Journal*, 4 (March 1967), 117-124.
11. Horn, Ernest. *Methods of Instruction in the Social Studies*. New York: Scribner's, 1937, 166.
12. James, Preston E., and Nelda Davis. *The Wide World: A Geography*. New York: Macmillan, 1959, 124-125.
13. Lloyd, Donald J. "Reading American English Sound Patterns," *Monograph for Elementary Teachers No. 104*. Evanston, Illinois: Row, Peterson, 1962, 2.
14. Postman, Neil, and Charles Weingartner. *Linguistics: A Revolution in Teaching*. New York: Dell, 1967, 139.
15. *Ibid.*, 141-153.
16. Preston, Ralph C. *Teaching Social Studies in the Elementary School* (3rd ed.). New York: Holt, Rinehart and Winston, 1968, 293-295.
17. Preston, Ralph C. "The Multiple-Choice Test as an Instrument in Perpetuating False Concepts," *Educational and Psychological Measurement*, 25 (Spring 1965), 111-116.
18. Preston, Ralph C., J. Wesley Schneyer, and Franc J. Thyng. *Guiding the Social Studies Reading of High School Students*. Washington, D. C.: National Council for the Social Studies, 1963.
19. Toynbee, Arnold J. *A Study of History*. New York: Oxford, 1947, 319.

Reading and Controversial Issues

JAMES P. SHAVER
Utah State University

IT IS OBVIOUS that reading has a great deal to contribute to the study of controversial issues. A considerable amount of time could be spent in discussing such matters as where to locate appropriate, current reading materials for the study of controversy, how to take reading level into account in assigning reading about controversial issues, and how to tie readings into discussions of controversy. This paper is, however, concerned with two other aspects of reading and controversial issues: (1) What role might controversy play in motivating students to read? and (2) Once students are reading, what sort of intellectual framework should be taught for reading about controversy?

The first question, which is concerned with getting students at all age levels to read so that they will develop the habit of reading and learn basic reading skills, will be treated briefly in the first part of the paper. The second, more extensive, part of the paper will deal with "higher level" reading skills—the "critical reading" skills which must be taught if the engagement of students in reading is to make a rational contribution to the consideration of controversy. Both topics will, of course, be discussed from the perspective of a social studies curriculum developer, rather than that of a reading specialist. If the ideas presented have validity, however, they will have import for the teacher of reading, as well as for the social studies teacher who is concerned with reading as it relates to his objectives in the social studies.

Reading Must Have Purpose

It is important to begin a consideration of reading and controversial issues by recognizing that the purposes which guide the student's school-related behavior are often on two significantly different levels. One level of purpose is simply to meet the formal requirements of the classroom

Author's note: Many of the ideas discussed in this paper have been developed through research performed pursuant to a contract with the United States Department of Health, Education, and Welfare, Office of Education. Critiques by A. Guy Larkins and Morris Mower of drafts of the paper have been especially helpful.

in order to get a decent grade and stay out of trouble. Much reading is done for that purpose, but many reading assignments go undone because formal school requirements are the only motivation. A second level of purpose for the students is to find meaning, to construe and understand the world around them. Here, controversy and reading bear a close relationship.

Is the school "real"?   Why do students often see little meaning in school assignments beyond the meeting of superficial requirements? School undoubtedly is for a great many students an artificial, sterile environment. The school is a conservative institution. In most communities, in fact, school officials try to isolate the school from controversy. School people themselves tend to be rather quiet, uncontroversial figures. (If they were not, they would likely lose their jobs in many instances.) The administrative framework of the school is typically used to enforce conformity rather than encourage diversity or controversy over even such trivial matters as clothing and hair styles.

The curriculum itself is often not just noncontroversial but of little relevance to the student's life. Literature classes, for example, are often magnificently irrelevant in their emphasis on the "great works," regardless of their limited interest for the students. (Some experiences with a tutorial program for underachieving readers (*26*) indicate that even putting a "classic" in paperback format does not necessarily make it interesting— although it may help.) Many English departments are using readings which are more relevant to the students' lives, but in some cases the public outcry against books such as *Catcher in the Rye* or *Black Like Me* has involved the school in the controversy which is anathema to many school administrators. Elementary reading texts, too, with all of their blandness, must often seem irrelevant to the beginning reader who sees a more exciting and disputatious world around him. Apparently in an attempt to insult no one, beginning reading books often lack even the entertainment quality of, for instance, the Dr. Suess books which commonly introduce children to reading in economically (or educationally) affluent homes.

Perhaps, however, curricular sterility is present most of all in the social studies. Social studies teachers commonly emphasize history for its own sake. Despite pleas to the contrary in professional journals (*11*), history books are rarely based on any rationale other than chronology. U.S. history courses which have time for current history undoubtedly exist, but they are rare. And, textbooks are often confused in their treatments of the place of diversity in society (*23*).

It is questionable if the "new social studies" will do much to alleviate the situation. Educators continue to maintain a confused stance in regard to whether they are teaching a social studies or a social science curriculum (*25*). One of the major thrusts in social studies curriculum development has been an emphasis on the structures of the disciplines, including how to "think like an historian" (*12, 21*). And, too few social studies educators have asked whether the structures which are meaningful to the scientist, or to the teacher, help students to give meaning to their environment (*27*). Consequently, much of the "new social studies" continues an emphasis on abstract intellectual exercises with little concern for relevance to students enrolled in a general education program required of all, and suffered by many.

In short, the school generally ignores the realities of life surrounding the student. Controversy abounds and is a basic fact of the student's life. He is often in conflict with his parents, with his peers, with the school—if only because of their commitment to conformity and agreement. And, especially because of the rapid communication in the electronics era, it must be clear to most students that controversy and disagreement are basic elements in the political life of society.

Controversy—A Curricular Focal Point

Perhaps it would be unrealistic, even foolish, to propose that the entire school curriculum be centered on controversy—although it seems within the realm of reason to suggest that the school as an institution should be much more open to dialogue about controversial matters. It also seems reasonable to propose that the social studies curriculum in particular should take controversy as its focal point.

Social studies educators have assumed prime responsibility for citizenship education in the school. While this is not the place to elaborate on the point, it seems clear that, in a democratic society committed to individual participation in political decisions made within a pluralistic framework, controversy is inevitable (*22*). The recognition, toleration, and rational handling of controversy certainly are appropriate goals for a curriculum committed to citizenship education (*20*).

There is considerable evidence that students are interested in the basic issues facing society; that, at least by junior high school age, they can deal with these issues without suffering psychological harm; and that subject matter will take on more meaning when it is related to the study of basic issues (*20*). Reading material bearing on the divisive issues facing society might well establish the relevance, the purpose for reading that has been lacking for many students.

What kind of reading? The basic proposition to this point is, then, that attention to controversy can increase students' reading activities by making the curriculum relevant to life. The traditional view of reading as a source of information and ideas for dealing with controversy is valid, but involvement in controversy can also provide a meaningful context and motivation for reading.

It should be obvious that if reading is to be done in the context of understanding and grappling with controversy, a broad definition of reading is implied. Certainly, word recognition or repetition is not sufficient, nor is comprehension or retention. If reading is to be maximally useful to the student in his analysis of controversy, the definition of reading must be nearly synonymous with that for thinking (17, 18). Yet as Berlak (2) has pointed out, the appropriateness of a model of critical thinking depends upon the context in which it is to be used. So it is incumbent upon the teacher (or curriculum developer) to specify the context within which he wants his students to read critically.

What kind of controversy?   A specification of context must begin by asking what kind of controversy we are interested in having our students learn to analyze. There are many types and levels of controversy. There is controversy over esthetic matters such as taste in music and dress, controversy in the family over such matters as responsibility for chores, personal controversy over such questions as how much effort to put out in school or whether to go to school at all, and classroom controversy over concerns such as the proper amount of homework. Each of these types of controversy may be of great importance to the individuals involved, but does any one provide the proper focal point for shaping reading behavior?

In light of the citizenship education commitment of social studies education already menioned, it probably makes sense to distinguish between private and public controvesy—the first involving those issues which are a matter of personal concern and the second involving those issues which are a matter of public debate and policy making. The former are better left to the counseling department and to the homemaking and music appreciation courses; the latter must be of concern in the social studies if the curriculum is to be relevant to the student's coming role as citizen. Of course, the question of which matters are public issues and which are private is itself open to debate, as has been pointed out elsewhere (20: 57-58).

Once a decision has been made that controversy over public issues is what is to be of concern, a first major step has been taken in delineating the frame of reference from which to help students learn to read. We will want to be concerned with writings relevant to the major questions under debate in society, currently or perennially. And, we will want to teach appropriate analytic concepts to be brought to bear on those reading materials. It is to this second concern that this paper will now be addressed in some detail, for it is obviously not a sufficient basis for instruction to say simply that students must be taught to read critically about public issues.

Intellectual Skills for Reading about Public Issues

As already noted, Berlak (2) has contended that general models of thinking may not be of much use in thinking about problems in specific contexts. He maintains that educators should study the intellectual demands of particular problem areas and build "context-specific" models, with attendant teaching strategies and materials. If his thesis is correct, and it is hoped that the following discussion will help to validate his point, then we must ask if taking controversy over public issues as a pivotal concern provides cues as to which intellectual skills will be particularly appropriate for a "critical reading" model. In a sense this question may be seen as asking whether the typical emphasis on an oversimplified approach (29) to problem solving qua scientific method on historical inquiry or on propaganda analysis is adequate (8, 24).

Identifying disagreement over public issues as the type of controversy of concern is a good starting point in the quest for appropriate concepts of "critical reading," but it is not sufficient. An analysis on the nature of public issues is also necessary. It is, for example, important to recognize that public issues generally involve policy questions which are basically ethical in nature; that is, public debate is commonly over issues which have to do with proper aims for the society and proper conduct for the individuals and agencies in the society. Once one has settled on this basic fact of public controversy, the context has been set for further analysis and the identification of concepts to be applied to reading about controversy. A brief sketch of the results of such an analysis and identification follows. It will touch upon the reader's evaluation of factual claims, value analysis in reading about controversy, and some concepts in regard to language which can assist in critical reading.

Facts and controversy.   Obviously, facts are relevant to settling societal-ethical questions (which might better be called political-ethical questions because public issues tend to be settled finally in the political domain of society). What one thinks *should* be done (for example, in regard to a proposal to reduce *de facto* segregation by bussing students) often depends upon the answers to factual questions. These may be about the past (Has there been a history of denial of equal education to Negroes?), about the present (Are rapid gains being made in making schools in predominantly Negro neighborhoods equal to schools in other neighborhoods?), in regard to what can be done (Is there an adequate tax base for increased bus costs?), and about possible consequences (Will the level of education actually be raised? What will be the effects on the attitudes of Negro and white children? How will white and Negro parents react?) The answers to such questions require a base of information.

Reading has commonly, and legitimately, been seen as a valuable source of such information.

In fact, the citizen is much more like the historian than like the social scientist in his attempts to find out about the facts of public controversy. Like the historian, the citizen must rely almost exclusively on secondary sources of information. One knows about Vietnam, about the riots in Detroit, and about the medical officer who refuses to train Green Berets primarily through the reports of others. Rarely does one interview participants in controversy or carry out research of one's own, in the social science sense of experimentation, to gather data. One relies on newspapers, magazines, books, and, of course, radio and television.

The evaluation of sources of information has been a fairly common topic (6). Lists such as the following taken from our own project work (33) are not unusual:

1. Questions to ask about the observations upon which statements to be used as evidence have been based:
   a. Has the observer the relevant expertise, based on education or experience, to make the required observations?
   b. What biases or sets does the observer have that might have affected his observations?
   c. Was the observer's emotional state such that it might have interfered with or influenced his observations?
   d. Does the observer have a history of accurate observations?
   e. Do the observations agree with those of other independent observers?
2. Questions to be asked of the report:
   a. What are the time and space relationships between the reporter, the event, and the statement of the event?
      (1) Was the reporter an eye witness, or is he reporting on the basis of someone else's observations?
      (2) If the reporter was not an eye witness, does he tell who his source is?
      (3) If the reporter is not an eye witness, is his source (or sources) reliable?
      (4) If the reporter was not an eye witness, did he get his information directly from an eye witness?
      (5) How soon after his observation of the event or after being told about the event did the reporter make his statement about it?
   b. What biases does the reporter have—judging from his background, from his group affiliations, from his choices of words, from the publication in which the report is made—that *might* affect his reporting?
   c. Have the means of presenting data (charts and graphs, statistics used) affected the picture given?
   d. Does the report agree with other independent reports?

Underlying concepts.   If, however, such lists are to be functional for the student in his reading, he must also have a foundation of other concepts. For example, he should be aware that individuals have a need for an orderly world. Disorder is not only uncomfortable, it is unmanageable. Some understanding of the dynamics of maintaining an orderly world is also important. For example, young people should know that one way to maintain order is through *perceptual sets (28)*. ("Set" is not intended in the sense of neural responses, but in the sense of expectations based on our experiences and needs which assist us in selecting and ordering the many stimuli around.) The student should recognize that although organizing tools, such as perceptual sets, are essential to our functioning, they can also limit the validity of our data. And, the student should experience some of the limitations imposed by his own perceptual sets so that he can better appreciate how they may limit the data gathered and reported by others, as well as how they affect his own intake of those data.

Other important concepts, also based on the notion of our need for orderliness, have to do with the way in which we handle inconsistencies in our beliefs and information. Just as disorder is uncomfortable, so is inconsistency *(4, 13)*. Individuals develop a number of irrational ways of maintaining consistency that are especially related to reading. We tend to avoid, deny, and/or distort sources of information which are inconsistent with our beliefs. Recognition that a need for orderliness affects our own view of the world provides an excellent basis for evaluating the observations and the reports of others.

Types of factual claims.   Categorizations of the types of claims in reports will also help the student to be properly analytic in his controversy-related reading. Many claims about the facts relevant to societal issues are specific claims—assertions about what occurred at a particular time and place. The student should be aware, however, that people more commonly make general factual claims (generalizations) based on a number of specific claims or on other general factual claims. The student should learn to break general claims into the various more specific claims upon which they are based and to examine these for their validity.

Some knowledge of sampling procedures can also be helpful in analyzing general factual claims. Writers frequently deal with samples of social events as well as samples of people, and it is important that students know appropriate questions—both as to numbers and selection processes—to ask about the adequacies of the samples upon which generalizations are based.

Assumptions.   Just as assumptions about the adequacy of samples must be questioned, so must other assumptions underlying the claims in written reports be explicated and critically examined. For example, an erroneous assumption that correlation demonstrates cause and effect commonly leads to invalid claims. Other common, but incorrect, assumptions have to do with the relationships between group and individual characteristics—that what is. true of a group will be true of each individual in the group (fallacy of division) and that what is true of the individuals making up the group will be true of the group as an entity (fallacy of composition). These fallacies, or erroneous assumptions, are commonly treated in logic textbooks (*3, 7, 15*), although not in elementary or secondary school textbooks. Also frequently present in writings about public issues are the assumptions that a complex social occurrence has only one cause and that past or present trends will continue into the future. Huff (*16*) has dealt with a number of the assumptions to be taken into account in evaluating quantitative data reported in written form.

Analogies.   Obviously, all of the concepts that might be used in evaluating written sources of information cannot be discussed in a brief paper. One other topic should be touched upon, however, because it illustrates the importance of developing a model of critical reading that is specific to the context of controversy over public issues.

Treatments of "reflective thinking" in social studies textbooks are commonly based on a model which involves identifying a problem, formulating a hypothesis, and then gathering evidence to prove or disprove the hypothesis and thus "solve" the problem (*24*). As will be pointed out shortly, this model ignores the basic role of values in coming to acceptable solutions to problems. It also ignores the situational context within which one commonly deals with public issues.

Rarely in the analysis of public issues can we set up a hypothesis and gather specific data bearing directly on it. Instead, we find ourselves frequently arguing, or being argued to, by analogy. Should we be fighting in Vietnam? Many arguments about this question hinge on the appropriateness of an analogy between what happened after Munich and what might happen in Southeast Asia (*34*). Is it possible to set up instances in which "aggression" is not met with force in order to determine what the consequences are likely to be? Of course not. Nor can precisely relevant data be gathered via interviews, questionnaires, or the other common paraphernalia of the social sciences. So concerned people find themselves looking for other situations, analogous cases, which will give some basis for arguing the probable outcome of different policies or actions. This situation is as true in dealing with domestic problems, each one of which tends to be unique in many critical respects, as it is with international problems. Glibly stated analogies are too often readily accepted as proof of the consequences likely to follow or not to follow advocated policies.

It is unfortunate, therefore, that argument by analogy has not been a part of the common "critical thinking" schemes which have served as the basis for critical reading (*18: Part 2*). In particular, students who will be reading materials treating controversial topics should be able to recognize arguments by analogy and identify the two (or more) cases which the author is assuming to be analogous, as these are often not clearly stated. Then students should be able to analyze the differences and similarities in the cases and make judgments about their importance in terms of the probability that what occurred in one instance is likely to occur in the other.

Values and reading about public issues. Factual claims are important to controversy over public issues, and "critical reading" must be oriented to the evaluation of the trustworthiness of information, accompanied by caution about our own "filtering" of what is read. However, the recognition that controversy over societal issues is basically a matter of ethical dispute—disagreement over proper aims and actions—opens to consideration another important aspect of reading.

The relevance to public controversy of values—standards or principles of worth and ideas as to what is good, worthwhile, or desirable—has often been overlooked in the social studies curriculum. As a matter of fact, Ennis (*10*), in presenting a schema of critical thinking that is frequently cited as the basis for curriculum work, explicitly excluded value choices to make his list of concepts more manageable. There are scholarly bases for maintaining that value questions may be more difficult than factual questions to handle reflectively and that the same techniques will not be applicable to both (*30, 31*). This condition does not excuse the failure of popular discussions of critical thinking to treat values as they relate to the making of political-ethical decisions. In fact, the exclusion is serious because proposed decisions to handle controversial issues are typically defended in terms of values. How else is one ultimately to defend a position, except to argue that it will support or enhance those things that people consider worthwhile? Facts cannot finally tell us what ethical choice to make. The facts pertinent to an issue may be agreed upon—for example, that a certain policy would give Negroes more nearly equal education and also lead to miscegenation. Yet, there is still likely to be considerable disagreement over whether the policy should be executed. Whether one positively values equality of education and/or miscegenation would be a critical factor in a decision to support or oppose the policy.

This is not the place to develop a detailed account of how values function in relation to political-ethical decisions in this society. Such a discussion is available elsewhere (*20*). It should be noted, however, that, as might be implied from the education-miscegenation example, the relationship of values to decisions is a complex one. Rarely does making a decision involve simply identifying the "correct" value and acting in accord with it.

Value conflict. As Myrdal (*19*) has pointed out in *An American Dilemma*, the general values of society often conflict with evaluations of specific situations. A man might, for example, believe that all men should have equal economic opportunity and yet feel that it was perfectly all right not to hire Negroes in his plant because "that's the policy." However, the general values of society also conflict with one another as one attempts to apply them to the defense of proposals and action vis-a-vis public issues. A classic example is the conflict between freedom and equality; the extension of one often means limitation of the other. The reminder that one cannot have one's cake and eat it too is particularly pertinent to public issues. One cannot, for instance, force men into the armed services against their will and maintain unsullied freedom of conscience (or vice versa). Difficult choices must be made.

Often, then, action predicated on one important societal value will involve the denial of another important value. In a pluralistic society, conflict over values becomes inevitable as individuals and groups with varying backgrounds and orientations emphasize different value positions and interpret values differently when proposing and opposing solutions to the problems facing society. Of course, because the individual is committed to the general values of society, the value conflict is intrapersonal as well as interpersonal.

Reading and values. What does the role of values in controversy have to do with reading? To begin with, the student reader should learn that each person has a frame of reference, a set of beliefs, about what the world is like, can be like, and *should* be like (*1*) and that this frame is an important determinant of behavior. In reading, he should learn to examine discussions of public issues in terms of the societal values which are implied or explicitly stated. He should ask whether a policy being propounded is defended in terms of the basic values of the society or in terms of the narrower, more parochial elements of the writer's frame of reference. If the writer does not state the societal values underlying his position, the student should be able to identify relevant values and analyze the proposal in terms of them. This task involves asking which value or values support the proposed policy and which oppose it or, conversely, which values would be enhanced by the decision and which denegated.

Value analysis in reading, then, involves the explicit search for and explication of conflicting values so that they can be weighed in evaluating the writer's position. The intellectual strategies for resolving value conflicts are important to the adequate conceptualization of a social studies curriculum geared to controversy, but that goes beyond a paper on reading and controversial issues to one aimed more explicitly at decision-making.

Language—a basic element. Last, but not least, in a discussion of critical reading concepts for the study of controversy some attention is due language, which, as the basic means of communication, is the intermediary between the writer and the reader. It is obvious that learning to read must involve attention to words and the way in which they are put together to convey meaning. If one approaches reading instruction from the viewpoint of the intellectual skills appropriate to reading about controversial issues, it is evident that the student must have, as a foundation for critical reading, a firm understanding of the role and nature of language. He must be aware that language is basic to communication and thinking but that our use of language provides pitfalls in our attempts to deal with controversy rationally (*5, 14*).

Words, like the other conventions of a society, tend to take on a certain mysticism. Our words often seem "natural"; other languages sound strange. And, the relations between many words and their referents seem somehow inherent: after all, they are the only word referent relationships with which many individuals are familiar. Consequently, a good beginning point in assisting the student to become a more rational reader is to make him aware that words are symbols and that, as with other symbol referent relationships, word referent relationships are conventions adopted by men, not qualities of the words.

With this understanding, the student will be able to comprehend that the important question to be asked of an author's choice of words is not "Is he using the 'correct word'?" but "What meaning is he trying to convey through his choice of words?" In short, with shifts in word meaning common over the years and with new words being invented continually (*32*), the student should recognize that it is more functional to be concerned with communication than with conventional correctness.

Emotive meaning.   In searching out the intended message of the writer, the student should be acutely aware that words carry both descriptive and emotive meaning; that is, words convey information, but they also convey and arouse emotion. Literature courses often deal with the emotions aroused by writings as one positive aspect of a creative effort by an author or an esthetic response by a reader. In teaching reading for controversial issues, however, it is appropriate to be concerned with the dangers rather than the esthetics or the literary contributions of emotive loading. For the emotive loadings of words can influence us to accept or reject claims or to agree or disagree with a position. Furthermore, if negative emotive loading becomes too strong, if the words used are too abhorrent to the reader, communication may break down. For example, the use of profanity or the admission by the author that he is a "communist" or "John Bircher" will lead some people to quit reading an article or book. Clearly, an understanding of how perceptual sets function and of how one tends to handle dissonant information in irrational ways would provide an excellent frame for evaluating reactions to emotively loaded words.

The use of emotion in language is especially likely to occur when authors make value statements. Some of the common categories of propaganda are related to value-laden language—for example, "glittering generalities." In fact, if the student can identify emotively loaded language and avoid its effects (a task which no one can do entirely), as well as explicate and evaluate assumptions in controversy-related reading, he has acquired the basic thrust of propaganda analysis.

It should be noted that the difficulties of communication are much greater in some respects in reading than in face-to-face oral discourse. There is, of course, always a possibility in oral discussions that the "personalities" of the discussants will interfere with communication; people sometimes react to mannerisms rather than to words. Moreover, discussion usually does not allow the time for reflection that reading does. Nevertheless, discussion has the major advantage that one can ask the speaker what he meant to say. Discussion allows for a process of clarification and definition which simply is not possible in reading, unless the written communication is part of a sequence of correspondence. This statement does not mean that reading is any less valuable than discussion; in fact, each can make invaluable contributions to the other. It does mean, however, that the reader must be intensely aware that reading is a process of one-way communication with many possibilities for breakdowns in communication of which either the writer or reader may be unaware.

Summary and Conclusions

This paper has had two major objectives in regard to reading and controversial issues. The first was to suggest that controversy has a contribution to make to the motivation of reading. It was argued that a curriculum which recognizes and focuses on controversy is likely to be more relevant to the student than is the typical school curriculum; and the reading which is a part of that curriculum is likely to take on purpose beyond the fulfillment of formal school requirements. It was proposed that the social studies curriculum, in particular, should center on controversy over the proper policies in regard to those issues which are a matter of public debate and political solution.

The second major objective had to do with the proposition that instruction for reading about controversy must center on critical reading and that the selection of concepts for critical reading instruction must be contingent upon an analysis of that controversy toward which the curriculum is intended to affect behavior. The remainder of the paper elaborated on this point by sketching some concepts that are particularly appropriate for critical reading about public issues controversy. The discussion of the analytic concepts was necessarily brief and not meant to be exclusive. Using public issues as the context, the intent has been to indicate the dimensions which might structure an attempt to delineate critical reading.

Clearly, two tasks need to be accomplished before suggestions such as those in this paper can be put into operation by the classroom teacher. First the critical reading concepts need to be stated more specifically and in a format which can serve readily for the development of materials and procedures for teaching the concepts. That development comprises the second task. The Utah State University Social Studies Project (*33*) has been aimed at both of these tasks, but with a general concern for the analysis of public issues extending beyond critical reading. The charge to specify and organize concepts as a basis for curriculum development and then to develop the means by which to teach them necessitates a time-consuming undertaking, one that demands resources that are usually beyond the means of a single teacher. It does seem evident, however, that we are not likely to produce the critical, rational students which our objectives claim until crucial concepts are enumerated, materials are designed specifically for teaching those concepts, and the rationale for the selection of the concepts and the resulting materials becomes an integral part of the school curriculum.

Where in the curriculum?   At this point, a question might legitimately be raised as to which "curriculum" is being referred to. Controversy and the analytic concepts for controversy-related reading have not been discussed in this paper in terms of elementary or secondary school levels of curriculum. Instead, it has been assumed that centering on controversy and the analytic concepts for dealing rationally with controversy is appropriate at all grade levels. Instruction for critical controversy-related reading is not likely to be very effective if left to the senior year course in problems of democracy, into which specific concern for citizenship education is often placed in schools. There should be a cumulative program, beginning in grade school and building through the high school.

Certainly, elementary school students can be introduced to the idea of disagreement as an essential element in democracy (as they well know it is in their own lives). And, very early in the elementary years such concepts as the fallibility of our senses can be taught. By the time the student is in the eighth grade, he should have been introduced to the full range of a set of concepts such as discussed in this paper. A good share of the social studies curriculum during the high school years should be aimed at developing a more complex understanding of the concepts and their applicability. As soon as possible, the students should be involved in the application of the "critical reading" concepts to the issues confronting the society. Of course, this phase will take place concurrently with the application of social science concepts which should also be taught in the general education program as part of understanding and dealing rationally with public issues.

A proposal for a cumulative curriculum calls, of course, for curricular articulation from kindergarten through grade twelve. This prerequisite, which seems so obvious, has been almost totally lacking in the social studies curriculum in most school districts and even within individual schools. Such articulation requires not only a specification of objectives in terms of the concepts to be learned by the students but decisions by the professional staff as to the grade levels at which various concepts or the understandings leading to various concepts can and should be taught. This type of programing seems to have been an impossible task in the social studies, as contrasted, for example, with mathematics where the developmental nature of the subject matter seems more obvious. Articulation in terms of overall curricular goals is among the most pressing business for social studies educators.

Other aspects of the question "Which curriculum?" need to be touched upon. This paper has assumed an audience of social studies educators interested in reading. At the secondary level, social studies teachers are not typically concerned with basic reading skills, and the emphasis on "critical" reading is, perhaps, obviously appropriate. At the elementary school level any one teacher is likely to be responsible for basic reading instruction *and* social studies instruction. There is no intent in this paper to suggest that critical reading should supplant the teaching of basic reading skills. Instead, the two should supplement each other. For example, attention to controversy might assist in teaching reading fundamentals by leading some teachers from the innocuous beginning-reading texts which are not likely to generate much excitement about reading. At the same time, attention to rudimentary concepts of critical reading can accompany the teaching of basic reading skills.

The elementary teacher is often responsible for subjects other than reading and social studies. In this situation, articulation among subject areas is easier than at the secondary level. The science portion of the elementary school curriculum can, if it is concerned at a simple level with the processes and difficulties of scientific investigation (9), contribute to the child's understanding of the shortcomings of his own senses and, thereby, make a contribution to critical reading. In the later school years, contact between the social studies teacher's attempts to teach critical thinking and the English teacher's attempts to do the same is extremely important; for as already noted, learning to read controversy-related material analytically is not something which is accomplished in the course of a semester in isolation from the rest of the student's school program.

Nor, as already emphasized at great length, is the model of critical thinking which underlies the teaching of critical reading likely to be adequate unless it is based on careful consideration of the type of controversy about which the students are being prepared to read. For the social studies, with its longstanding concern for citizenship education, controversy over public issues seems to be a strikingly appropriate focal point. And, it is crucial for an adequate frame of analysis that public issues be recognized as basically ethical issues with values playing an eminent role in the justification of any proposed policy or action.

References

1. Beard, Charles. *The Nature of the Social Sciences.* New York: Charles Scribner's Sons, 1934, 178-184.
2. Berlak, Harold. "The Teaching of Thinking," *School Review,* 73 (Spring 1965), 1-13.
3. Black, Max. *Critical Thinking: An Introduction to Logic and Scientific Method* (2nd ed.). New York: Prentice-Hall, 1952.
4. Brown, Roger. *Social Psychology.* New York: Free Press, 1965, Chapter 11.
5. Chase, Stuart. *Power of Words.* New York: Harcourt, Brace and World, 1954.
6. Clark, Nadine. *A Guide to Effective Critical Thinking.* New York: Macmillan, 1965.
7. Copi, Irving M. *Introduction to Logic.* New York: Macmillan, 1961.
8. Dewey, John. *How We Think.* Boston: Heath, 1933.
9. Elementary School Science Project. *Science for First Grade: A Manual for Teachers.* Logan, Utah: Utah State University, 1964.
10. Ennis, Robert H. "A Concept of Critical Thinking," *Harvard Educational Review,* 32 (Winter 1962), 81-111.
11. Feder, Bernard. "A Study of the Past Focused on the Present," *Social Education,* 32 (October 1968), 529-578.
12. Fenton, Edwin, and John Good. "Project Social Studies: A Progress Report," *Social Education,* 29 (April 1965), 206-208.
13. Festinger, Leon. *A Theory of Cognitive Dissonance.* Evanston, Illinois: Row, Peterson, 1957.
14. Hayakawa, S. I. *Language in Thought and Action,* (2nd ed.). New York: Harcourt, Brace, and World, 1964.
15. Hepp, Maylon H. *Thinking Things Through: An Introduction to Logic.* New York: Charles Scribner's Sons, 1956.
16. Huff, Darrell. *How to Lie with Statistics.* New York: W. W. Norton, 1954.
17. Huus, Helen. "Reading," in Helen McCracken Carpenter (Ed.), *Skill Development in Social Studies.* Washington, D. C.: National Council for the Social Studies, Thirty-third Yearbook, 1963, Chapter 6.

18. King, Martha L., Bernice D. Ellinger, and Willavene Wolf (Eds.). *Critical Reading.* Philadelphia: J. B. Lippincott, 1967.
19. Myrdal, Gunnar. *An American Dilemma: The Negro Problem and Modern Democracy.* New York: Harper and Brothers, 1944, xlvii-xlix, 1027-1031.
20. Oliver, Donald W., and James P. Shaver. *Teaching Public Issues in the High School.* Boston: Houghton Mifflin, 1966.
21. Schultz, Mindella. "The Scholar's Role in a Democratic Society," *Social Education,* 32 (October 1968), 534-538, 541.
22. Shaver, James P. "Americanism as an Educational Objective," *Educational Forum* (in press).
23. Shaver, James P. "Diversity, Violence, and Religion: Textbooks in a Pluralistic Society," *School Review,* 75 (Autumn 1967), 311-328.
24. Shaver, James P. "Reflective Thinking, Values, and Social Studies Textbooks," *School Review,* 73 (Autumn 1965), 226-257.
25. Shaver, James P. "Social Studies: The Need for Redefinition," *Social Education,* 31 (November 1967), 588-592, 595.
26. Shaver, James P., and Dee Nuhn. "Underachievers in Reading and Writing Respond to a Tutoring Program," *The Clearing House* (in press).
27. Shaver, James P., and Donald W. Oliver. "The Structure of the Social Sciences and Citizenship Education," in James P. Shaver and Harold Berlak (Eds.), *Democracy, Pluralism, and the Social Studies: Readings and Commentary.* Boston: Houghton Mifflin, 1968.
28. Smith, Helen K. (Ed.). *Perception and Reading,* Proceedings of the International Reading Association, Vol. 12, Part 4, 1967 (Copyright 1968).
29. Smith, Philip G. "How We Think: A Reexamination," *Educational Forum,* 31 (May 1967), 411-420.
30. Stevenson, Charles L. *Ethics and Language.* New Haven: Yale University Press, 1944.
31. Stevenson, Charles L. *Facts and Values.* New Haven: Yale University Press, 1963, Chapter 1.
32. Ullman, Stephen. *Words and Their Use.* New York: Hawthorne Books, 1951.
33. Utah State University Social Studies Project. "A Curriculum Focused on Thinking Reflectively about Public Issues." United States Office of Education, Project No. 6-2288, Logan, Utah.
34. White, Ralph K. "Misperception and the Vietnam War," *Journal of Social Issues,* Vol. 22, No. 3 (July 1966).

Primary Sources—Their Nature and use in the Teaching of History

MARK M. KRUG
University of Chicago

IT SEEMS REASONABLE to assume that an understanding of the nature of history as a discipline and of the historical method of investigation is essential for successful history instruction. It is also clear that the teaching of a succession of chronological masses of "facts" or the "covering" of historical periods is not teaching of history, at least not in my understanding of the word. Amassing unrelated data and dates is not teaching history but is a meaningless exercise in futility. History teaching consists of a series of investigations into the past behavior of human beings in all parts of the world, both in groups and as individuals. *Historia,* as understood by the fathers of the discipline, Herodotus and Thucydides, was an empirical investigation (available historical traces serving as the new materials for the inquiry) into the past.

Objectives of Historical Inquiry

The purpose of the historical inquiry and of learning and teaching history has not changed from the formulation of Thucydides who clearly saw the uses of history as making available to the readers an account of alternative ways in which past generations of men dealt with periods of stress and conflict or performed in periods of tranquility. The relative constancy of human nature and the benefit from such insights are, or ought to be, quite obvious.

Thucydides (9) put it this way in his introductory statement to *A History of the Peloponnesian War*:

> It will be enough for me, however, if these words of mine are judged useful by those who want to understand clearly the events which happened in the past and which, human nature being what it is, will, at some time or other and in much the same ways, be repeated in the future. My work is not a piece of writing designed to meet the taste of an immediate public, but was done to last forever.

History conceived as an inquiry into the past conducted by historians, each of whom collects his data and interprets them in his own way, cannot be taught as a definitive study of the arbitrarily defined periods of history, "ancient," "medieval," "modern." If history is concerned with questions like What happened? When did it happen? How did it happen? Why did it happen and with what effects?, then it has to be taught in the form of problems, trends, movements, interrelationships, and processes—but not periods. When dealing with problems or movements like "balance of power," "atomic stalemate," or "the revolution of rising expectations," historians obviously do not agree with one another in their analyses of the problems or in their conclusions. History writing or historiography bears witness to this constant dialogue in which historians argue, provoke, inspire, or insult one another. An understanding of this continuous dialogue among historians must become an essential part of the teaching of history.

It is unfair to expect history, taught as inquiry into the past, to provide the student with ready-made approaches and solutions to contemporary problems. Even neophyte historians delving into the past actions of men quickly discover that while man can be a rational being, he often individually and even more often collectively acts irrationally. A *reasonable* explanation of a historical event may well be all wrong, and an irrational one may be right. When dealing in the realm of motivation which is an essential part of any major historical investigation, the sorting out of motives of leaders of men becomes a complex task. Historians are apt to differ in their appraisals because their own predilections and prejudices play an important part in the formulation of their judgments.

But these are not futile exercises. On the contrary, students can learn alternative modes of behavior and reactions of leaders of men and nations. Students can apply this knowledge to the understanding of problems and issues of the contemporary world. Bridenbaugh (2) maintained that a historical perspective is essential to any intelligent, critical analyses of a contemporary issue. "We owe it," he wrote, "to the entire past, the past which supports us to understand it to the best of our abilities, and we owe it to the future to make this past understandable. Too few of us fully appreciate the manifold merits of historical perspective. It saves us from becoming astigmatic about current events of the recent past. The corrosive and softening effects of time cause events to shrink to something like their normal sizes."

The Use of Historical Sources

The teaching of history as an inquiry into the past presupposes the extensive use of historical sources, documents, letters, speeches, or art in the classroom. We are faced with a paradox on this issue. History teachers have been exhorted in recent years to use primary sources and the market is inundated with "documentary histories," but there is overwhelming evidence that in most classrooms the only "document" used is the textbooks. Why is it so?

There are several reasons for this situation which if analyzed and corrected may bring a salutary change. First, the use of source materials requires some knowledge about the nature and variety of historical materials and, above all, skill in using them. Many teachers, prodded by a principal or a speaker at a lecture or a workshop, have made a sincere effort to use a document but have found the results disappointing. If, for instance, the teacher distributes Washington's Farewell Address and then insists that the students, in rotation read and discuss the speech, most of the children will soon "turn off" and the experiment will be a failure both for the students and the teacher. The Farewell Address is a magnificent piece of oratory, but much of it is tedious. The most relevant parts of the speech, the only ones which can be discussed with great profit, are the paragraphs dealing with Washington's formulation of the principles of the foreign policy of the United States.

> In the execution of such a plan nothing is more essential than that permanent, inveterate antipathies against particular nations and passionate attachments for others should be excluded, and that in place of them, just and amicable feelings toward all should be cultivated . . . .
>
> Against insidious wiles of foreign influence (I conjure you to believe me, fellow citizens) the jealousy of a free people ought to be *constantly* awake, since history and experience prove that foreign influence is one of the most beneficial foes of republican government . . . .
>
> It is our true policy to steer clear of permanent alliances with any portion of the foreign world, so far, I mean, as we are now at liberty to do it: for let me not be understood as capable of patronizing infidelity to existing engagements. I hold the maxim no less applicable to public than to private affairs that honesty is always the best policy. . . .
>
> Harmony, and a liberal intercourse with all nations are recommended by policy, humanity, and interest. . . (5).

George Washington not only charted the course of America's foreign policy, he also had some profound comments on the responsibility of this nation to be an example to the rest of mankind. He said (6):

> Observe good faith and justice toward all nations. Cultivate peace and harmony with all. Religion and morality enjoin this conduct. And can it be said that good policy does not equally enjoin it? It will be worthy of a free, enlightened, *and at no distant period a great nation to give to mankind the magnanimous and too novel example of a people always guided by an exalted justice and benevolence.* Who can doubt that in the course of time and things the fruits of such a plan would richly repay any temporary advantages which might be lost by a steady adherence to it?

These paragraphs in the long address, excerpted and underlined, may serve as a starting point for a meaningful and illuminating discussion in which the following points, among others, may be raised:

What does the speech tell us about George Washington? His character? His condition and literary style? How does the content of the speech relate to the often expressed judgment of historians that George Washington, while a great leader and general, was not intellectually profound? The address lends itself exceptionally well to a discussion of past and current foreign policy of the United States. To what extent did the United States' foreign policy follow the principles laid down by George Washington? How does the present U.S. foreign policy square with those principles? Can any nation in our complex, ideologically diverse world, with nations possessing atomic and hydrogen bombs, "cultivate peace and harmony with all," make honesty the criterion of its conduct in foreign affairs, and "steer clear of permanent alliances"?

It is, of course, suggested that these questions not be answered or dealt with superficially but lead the students to in-depth inquiries followed by a dialogue based on their research findings.

Only a historical document can allow the students to understand an historical event or a personality on its own terms, at least as much as it is possible for a contemporary mind. The English historian, Alan Bullock (3), put this process in these terms:

> What the historian finds fascinating is to come as close as he can to the concrete and the individual, to try to get inside the skin of this man or group of men, Napoleon, Cromwell, the Jacobins or the Bolsheviks.

How does one, for instance, try to get into the skin of President McKinley, one of our most underrated presidents, and try to understand his role in the Spanish-American War and in the great national debate on the annexation of the Philippines? History textbooks, almost without exception, glibly assert that in April 1896 President McKinley recommended that Congress declare war on Spain.

The reading of the text of McKinley's message to Congress reveals that his was not a war message. In fact, McKinley, after describing the situation in Cuba and relating the pressure exerted by the United States on the Spanish government to grant at least some of the demands of the Cuban rebels, *concluded* his message with these two paragraphs (7):

> Yesterday, and since the preparation of the foregoing message, official information was received by me that the latest decree of the Queen Regent of Spain directs General Blanco, in order to prepare and facilitate peace, to proclaim a suspension of hostilities, the duration and details of which have not yet been communicated to me.

This fact, with every other pertinent consideration, will, I am sure, have your just and careful attention in the solemn deliberation upon which you are about to enter. If this measure attains a successful result, then our aspirations as a Christian, peace-loving people will be realized. If it fails, it will be only another justification for our contemplated action.

It is abundantly clear that this was not a war message. It was just the opposite. President McKinley, a man truly dedicated to peace and opposed to foreign adventures pressed upon him by the imperialist triumvirate of Theodore Roosevelt, Senator Henry Cabot Lodge, and Captain Alfred Mahon, asked Congress *not* to declare war but to wait until the results of the new Spanish policy in Cuba could be ascertained.

But Congress was neither patient nor peace loving. It responded to a mood of national war hysteria whipped up by the bellicose press and the war hawks, who dominated both the Senate and the House, and had no difficulty in disregarding McKinley's plea. It declared that a state of war with Spain existed.

Is there a better way to get into the skin of President William H. McKinley than to read with the students a statement he made to a delegation of Methodist ministers in which he explained how he finally, after weeks of intense soul searching, decided to recommend the annexation of the Philippines?

The President told the ministers (8):

When I realized that the Philippines had dropped into our laps, I confess I did not know what to do with them. I sought counsel from all sides—Democrats as well as Republicans, but got little help. I thought first we would take only Manila; then other islands, perhaps, also. I walked the floor of the White House night after night until midnight; and I am not ashamed to tell you, gentlemen, that I went down on my knees and prayed Almighty God for light and guidance more than one night. And one night late it came to me this way—I don't know how it was but it came: (1) That we could not give them back to Spain—that would be cowardly and dishonorable; (2) that we could not turn them over to France or Germany—our commercial rivals in the Orient; that would be bad business and discreditable; (3) that we could not leave them to themselves—they were unfit for self-government—and they would soon have anarchy and misrule over there worse than Spain's was; and (4) that there was nothing left for us to do but to take them all, and to educate the Filipinos, and uplift and Christianize them, and by God's grace do the best we could by them, as our fellow men for whom Christ died. And then I went to bed and went to sleep, and slept soundly, and the next morning I sent for the chief engineer of the War Department (our map maker) and I told him to put the Philippines on the map of the United States [pointing to a large map on the wall of his office] and there they are and there they will stay while I am President.

This document ought to help the students to debate a number of interesting points:

1. What does the document tell us about McKinley, the man and the
   President?
2. What does this document tell us about Presidential decision making? What about the awesome burden of the President who almost
   daily has to make the final decisions?
3. How valid was McKinley's reasoning on the fate of the Philippines
   in case the United States refused to annex them?
4. To what extent has the United States fulfilled the dream that
   McKinley had for the Philippines?
5. Why did the President make this statement to the group of ministers? What do you suppose was the reaction of the ministers to
   the President's statement?

Importance of a Document's Setting

However, the most important condition for the effective use of a historical document, a condition seldom even thought about, is the presentation
of the document in its proper setting. McKinley's message to Congress,
half-heartedly recommending a declaration of war on Spain, or Franklin
Delano Roosevelt's First Inaugural Address giving heart to the nation
in the throes of a depression, will have the desired impact only if preceded
by a brief, concise, and dramatic presentation of the circumstances surrounding these messages. Understanding the setting for a speech, letter,
or excerpt from a diary is an essential element in the use of sources. Consider, for example, the introduction of Lincoln's Farewell Address to a
class. The teacher would be well advised to precede the reading of this
remarkable address by a short but dramatically delivered lecture.

Soon after his election in 1870, Abraham Lincoln realized quite clearly
the tasks that lay before him. He received the largest number of votes of the
four candidates; but together the three other candidates, Douglas, Breckin-
ridge, and Ball, received a million votes more than Lincoln. Thus, only a
minority of voters elected Lincoln, and almost no votes were cast for him
in the entire South.

In those days presidents elected in November did not take office until
March. During the long and crucial months before his inauguration, the
President-elect remained at his home in Springfield, Illinois, finishing the
business of his law practice and receiving visitors from all over the country,
including thousands of office seekers who made his life quite miserable.
Not wanting to infringe on the authority of President Buchanan, Lincoln

was reluctant to offer solutions to the slavery crisis which was keeping the nation at a high pitch of tension. Helplessly he watched the Union being split assunder by the secession in December of Mississippi, Florida, Alabama, Georgia, and Louisiana, and of Texas in early February. Almost daily he received warnings that the "Copperheads" in Maryland and the District of Columbia would prevent his inauguration even if it meant his assassination.

Disregarding these warnings and forebodings, Abraham Lincoln decided to go to Washington by the longest possible route, taking twelve days, in order to see as many people as he could. After many weeks of self-enforced silence, he was eager to talk and listen to the people of the North who had elected him to the highest office in the land. Surrounded by a handful of friends, Lincoln arrived at the railroad station in Springfield to board his train. The day was cold and damp; the skies were overcast, and a steady bone-chilling drizzle fell. Mr. Lincoln wore a black coat, a top hat, and a shawl over his shoulders. Around the rear platform of the train stood a wet and rather gloomy crowd of friends and neighbors who had come to bid farewell to their illustrious native son. They, of course, expected to hear a few words of farewell from the man they knew and loved so well.

Mr. Lincoln mounted the platform and said (*1*):

My Friends: No one, not in my situation, can appreciate my feeling of sadness at this parting. To this place, and the kindness of these people, I owe everything. Here I have lived a quarter of a century and have passed from a young man to an old man. Here my children have been born, and one is buried. I now leave, not knowing when or whether ever I may return, with a task before me greater than that which rested upon Washington. Without the assistance of that Divine Being who ever attended him, I cannot succeed. With that assistance, I cannot fail. Trusting in Him who can go with me, and remain with you, and be everywhere for good, let us confidently hope that all will yet be well. To His care commending you, as I hope in your prayers you will commend me, I bid you an affectionate farewell.

The rain was falling harder and, as the engine whistle blew, Lincoln rather wearily entered his car. The people stood for a while in the rain watching the train pull out of the station before they slowly dispersed.

How does a teacher "teach" this moving speech? First, as we said, he must place the speech in a setting and in perspective; then after the proper mood of expectation is achieved, he could with benefit read the speech to the class while reflecting the sadness and the drama of the circumstances in which it was given.

The discussion can center on a number of points:

1. Why is the Farewell Address one of Lincoln's finest speeches?
2. What words or sentences added or detracted from the address would "improve" it?
3. Would a President-elect today refer to himself as an "old man"? What does this tell us about Lincoln and about our times?
4. What are the reasons and the significance of Lincoln's prophetic statement that he might never return alive to Springfield?
5. In what way was Lincoln's task more difficult and more complex than that which faced Washington?
6. Was Lincoln, while not a churchgoer, nevertheless a man of profound faith in God?
7. What passages in the speech mark it particularly as a literary masterpiece?

Documents as a Basis for Learning the Historian's Methods

The document can also be used to make clear to the students that a historian in an important sense investigates a complex event of the past like a well-trained detective investigates a crime. A historian, like a detective, must be able to evaluate the available clues; he must test the reliability of the evidence and guard against following misleading paths in his inquiry. This careful treading in the maze of contradictory, sometimes irrelevant data and information, ought to prove fascinating to the students. They can be trained to approach any document with a large dose of scepticism. When confronted with a diary entry or a letter, they ought almost automatically to ask whether the document was indeed written by the persons to whom it was attributed, whether the author knew the truth about the particular event under consideration, whether, if he knew the truth, he wanted or was at liberty to tell it, and whether the document was tampered with or edited.

In the study of the Civil War, for instance, it was quite interesting to one group of students to read both the original version of the entries Gideon Welles, Lincoln's Secretary of the Navy, made in his diary and the "corrected" versions he made years later.

It is obviously important to know whether the author of a letter had a reputation for veracity or whether he was a known liar and fabricator and what his particular prejudices and biases were. Obviously Cicero, defending his arbitrary execution of the leaders of the Colabinion conspiracy, can hardly be considered an unbiased source as to the danger that Cateline and his associates posed for the Roman Republic.

The same caution is indicated when the teacher uses accounts taken from books written even by great historians. It would of course make no sense to assume that the fascinating account in Macaulay's *History* of the trials conducted by Lord Chief Justice George Jeffreys is fair and accurate. In fact, a number of historians have made an excellent case for the assertion that much of the evidence used by Macaulay was incomplete or unreliable.

What remains to be said is that neither teachers nor students ought to be under any illusion that even an exhaustive historical inquiry making full use of historical sources and documents would lead to the discovery of *the* truth. No historical investigation can ever use *all* of the historical evidence available, and even most important is the fact that any conclusions concerning a past event, while based on some empirical evidence, must contain in it some elements of artistic imagination.

Shakespeare was a good research historian, but his reconstruction of the murder of Julius Caesar contains much of his creative imagination. A historian who has devoted his entire life to assidious research of the fall of Bastille will, when putting down his findings, add his own artistic imagination to the hard data he got from his prolonged search for the facts. Thus, even his account will not be the whole truth or nothing but the truth.

The answers of an honest historian (and a teacher of history) are probably not absolute or definitive. His conclusion is based on the best analysis he was able to make of his data, the latter always selected and analyzed with some intrusion of personal bias and imagination hopefully controlled by experience, learning, and high standards of scholarship.

These points of caution do not, of course, minimize the attractions of the study of history. On the contrary, they point out its potential for a vigorous and exciting intellectual endeavor.

There is one more important limitation that deserves attention. We have little evidence on much of the past, and the inquiry into those aspects of the past is therefore severely limited. There is little we can do about the fact that the only sources available on the Carthaginian War and on Hazdrubal and Hannibal are from obviously biased and partial Roman historians. For some reason the advanced Phoenicians of Carthage left us nothing in the way of written records about their heroic struggle against the mighty Rome.

Conversely, there are historical events, particularly great conflicts, which have left, if one may say so, too much evidence. It took all the skill of Barbara Tuchman (*10*) to make some sense of the over-abundance of materials on World War I and make *The Guns of August* a highly readable and basically sound book.

In an important sense, Jacob Burckhardt (*4*) was right when he said that history is a contemplation based upon sources. The way in which this contemplation is carried out is as important as the new data and the new insight yielded by the sources. Historical method and historical content can be separated only at great peril for the product of an historical investigation. The intelligent use of the historical method of investigation on carefully assembled sources can and ought to teach the students the particular ways, mores, attitudes, languages, and even the little jokes of the discipline of history. This combination of method and sources ought to teach the student the ways in which historians go about their work.

For what purpose? One can only make modest claims for history.

The knowledge of the occasional *wisdom* of generations past ought to give hope and encouragement to the learner. On the other hand, the knowledge of past blunders and follies of mankind in its attempts to organize a peaceful and livable society, may not prevent similar mistakes in the present or in the future; but it may well make the odds a bit more favorable. History, if taught with scholarship and imagination, can give the students and the teachers a link with past human experience to help them feel that their own relatively short span of life may have meaning of its own in relation to the generations past and to their contemporary experience.

References

1. Angle, Paul M. (Ed.). *The Lincoln Reader.* New Brunswick, New Jersey: Rutgers University Press, 1935, 309.
2. Bridenbaugh, Carl. "The Great Mutation," *American Historical Review,* 68 (January 1963), 315-331, 324.
3. Bullock, Alan. "The Historian's Purpose: History and Metahistory," in Hans Meyerhoff (Ed.), *The Philosophy of History in Our Time.* New York: Doubleday, 1959, 294.
4. Burckhardt, Jakob. *Force and Freedom: Reflections on History.* New York: Pantheon Books, 1943, Chapter 1.
5. Commager, Henry Steele. *Documents of American History,* Vol. 1. New York: Appleton-Century-Crofts, 1963, 173-174.
6. *Ibid.*
7. *Ibid.,* Vol. 2, p. 4.
8. Olcott, Charles S. *Life of William McKinley,* 2. Boston: Houghton Mifflin, 1916, 110-111.
9. Thucydides. *The History of the Peloponnesian War.* Baltimore: Penguin, 1954, 24.
10. Tuchman, Barbara. *The Guns of August.* New York: Macmillan, 1962.

Induction, Skepticism, and Refutation: Learning Through Criticism

STEPHANIE G. EDGERTON
New York University

QUITE BY ACCIDENT one evening while reading I found an interesting example of what might be interpreted as a "reading" problem. Let me relate the story to you, for among other reasons it may serve as a source of comfort when you face, as many of you do daily, the enormously complex and difficult task of trying to teach students of the social studies to read. I happen to have found the incident very exciting, for it stimulated thought about the reading process; and I am hopeful that in sharing it with you I may assist you in your quest to develop better readers.

When Distinguished Philosophers Read

Some years ago the philosopher Paul Arthur Schilpp began editing a series of books called the *Library of Living Philosophers*. The general idea of the series was to present an opportunity for philosophers to discuss the work of an eminent "living" philosopher by offering comments and criticisms on which this philosopher would then write comments in reply. The format for each volume included a brief intellectual autobiography, approximately twenty papers, and a response to these papers. One such volume had as its subject the philosophy of Bertrand Russell.

The perspectives of Bertrand Russell are known to many people in many walks of life. Russell has been vigorous as a disputant concerned with a wide range of social issues. His more academic interests have focused on the foundations of mathematics, the methodology of science, the constructions of language, and the workings of the human mind. Young philosophers, typically, are introduced to his work early in their schooling, at which time they are told of his unusual lucidity. In the minds of most

Author's note: The major influences on this paper are the studies of Karl R. Popper in logic and scientific methodology. J. Agassi, B. Fisher, H. J. Perkinson and Ronald Swartz offered helpful comments and criticisms.

philosophers Russell's clarity of expression enjoys competition only with the clarity of his famous friend and philosopher, G. E. Moore.

But an interesting thing occurred on the occasion of the Schilpp-Russell volume. Schilpp reports in the way of apology to the distinguished philosophers who wrote papers for the volume—no doubt after thorough study of the Russellian writings on the topics of their contributions—and to the future readers of the books that the brevity of Russell's replies are to his mind explained by a comment made by Russell to the editor in private conversation. Russell disclosed to Schilpp his surprise in finding after careful reading of the manuscripts of the twenty-one contributors that "over half of their authors had *not* understood" him. Schilpp tells us that "This fact amazed Mr. Russell all the more because he always thought that he had been making every effort to write clearly and to express his ideas in the briefest possible and most direct way" (*17*).

The question I wish to raise is how could this happen? How may we explain the failure of a number of distinguished philosophers to interpret with some degree of accuracy and appreciation the thought of another very distinguished philosopher renowned for his clarity of expression? And how could it be that men of superior competence in matters of logic, semantics, and epistemology—disciplines from which other scholars draw their rules of critical thinking (*5*) and, more recently, critical reading (*9*) —have difficulty reading critically? Are the problems of interpretation related to matters of logic? of semantics? of epistemology? and, if they are, in what ways?

I seem to have stumbled across a very interesting example, one which I would like to explore philosophically. In this case, playing the role of a philosophical explorer means playing the game of a theoretical capitalist. Theoretical explorations of this kind, of course, unlike those of such well-known adventurers as Sir Edmund Hillary, who as you recall has provided us with magnificent accounts of his mountain climbing and polar expeditions (*7, 8*), have wide latitude for error. Indeed, from my point of view, intellectual expeditions may profit greatly from bold conjecturing, followed by determined and deliberate quests for errors.

From the outset it should be understood, then, that I do not wish to claim for my remarks the fruits of the experimentalist. That is, the systematic testing of theories is not my forte. Those who engage in such activities will be the subject of my opening remarks.

Man the Theoretician

Psychologists, sociologists, anthropologists, social psychologists, among others, have been working for many decades to discover and test theoretical information bearing on the problems of how people learn, think, perceive, etc. Unfortunate as it may be, the fact remains that to date we have no "mindoscope." We do not know, as a matter of fact, how people learn or how people think; nor do we know how many ways people may learn or people may think. As brilliant and informative as are the theoretical contributions of such great social scientists as Freud, Malinowski, Marx, Skinner, and Piaget (to name a few), our theoretical poverty about people is fairly staggering.

Perhaps, no one suffers more from this social scientific void than members of the teaching profession. They are regularly asked to accomplish feats of "teaching-learning" with little or no assistance from science. That they have done as well as they have seems, at least to me, a tribute to their own theoretical talents, though admittedly most teachers do not see themselves as theoreticians.

Seeing oneself as a theoretician is helpful, I think, in understanding why even distinguished philosophers have difficulty reading the lucid Bertrand Russell. I wish to suggest that *man is a theoretical animal,* bringing to his reading his theories, his perspectives, his viewpoints, or his biases in the light of which he attempts to interpret the theories of other men. This is no small achievement, as I hope my example indicates.

The problem seems to be one of utilizing one's own theoretical frameworks to discover the theoretical frameworks of another. We seem to approach the written word with bundles of theoretical materials—generalizations at many levels of abstraction on various topics—from which we then select, in hope of discovering the theoretical underpinnings or assumptions of an author's prose. If we are lucky, the writer may state his problem for us, feed us cues, and offer us forms of rhetoric and other devices which will help us to select the *theoretical arenas* in which we may through trial and error cull and create theoretical statements which seem fitting as an interpretation.

When we have what seems to be a match between his theoretical frameworks and ours, we seem to need some form of feedback to check it out. While reading a book, paper, or whatever, the interaction is limited substantially between the author and us in such a way that we, as readers, must do most of the work. All we seem able to do is to look for cues which indicate that our interpretation is inconsistent with what the author says. Finding such a cue, we may alter our theoretically constructed interpretation to take account of it. In the situation of schooling, we may, of course, introduce a mediator into the process—a teacher. The teacher may assist the reader by raising questions which lead to the digging out of cues, which in turn stimulate the reconstruction of an interpretation. Advanced readers, like the distinguished philosophers, may play each of the roles themselves. And, presumably, beginning readers may learn to become advanced readers. Part of advancing one's reading acumen, if I am right, is the recognition that the reader and the read both come with perspectives.

Let me briefly analyze my intellectual activities of the past two paragraphs. What I seem to have offered are psychological and sociological speculations about the act of interpretation when reading. I talked about operations of the mind, a reconstruction of an author's viewpoint, and a form of group interaction. I made hypotheses—offered theories—about what may happen in a situation when one is reading or learning to read well. Interestingly, my activity parallels in some respects the work of many theorists of curriculum and instruction. Much of what happens when designing teaching-learning units seems to qualify as sociological activity—specifically, applied sociology. Psychological considerations are no doubt implicit, in the sense of theories of mind, in these processes. This analysis tempts me to suggest that educational researchers confound logic and psychology while doing a form of sociology. If this is the case, theorists of curriculum and instruction might be wise to look over the various schools of sociology for assistance in what they are doing.

My speculative comments apart, it is unfortunate that the psychological and sociological processes of interpretation still remain secrets to us. This condition should not, however, move us to treat them as if they were not; or to treat them as if they were something else. Borrowing ready made solutions to problems may, if we are not careful, get us into trouble. A case in point would be an adoption of the Baconian tradition of inductive scientific methodology as a learning technique (4). But let me make myself clear.

Speaking forcefully against human prejudice, Sir Francis Bacon outlined a methodology of knowledge gathering designed to eliminate human error. But in the designing, Bacon seems to have eliminated too much. Seeing man as the holder and creator of *false* theories, he expelled from scientific activity man the theoretician. Eager to remove error from our scientific investigations, he lost sight of our greatest potential for knowledge—the creative powers of human beings. He traded a most imposing scientific resource, men's minds, for one of the products of their genius—a seemingly foolproof *logic of inquiry*. And I wish to stress that this exchange was done in the name of the doctrine of "pure" objectivity which was, incidentally, a prejudice of his own.

Bacon did not see that the question of how and where we get our ideas is different from and must be separated from the question of how we evaluate them. When we do not make the distinction between the *origins or sources* of our theories and *evaluations* of them (15), we shortchange ourselves in terms of viewing man's creative potentials. At the same time, we support barriers and erect blockades to an adequate analysis of the processes of inquiry. A glaring example of this confusion is the refusal by many to accept "intuition" as a source of theoretical information. Interestingly, this old and venerable notion has recently come into its own in the description scientists and those who study the activities of scientists give us (*13, 14, 15, 16, 18*).

The inadequacies of our sociopsychological theoretical explanations which are related to the problem of interpretation must not, on the other hand, prohibit us from guessing at the solutions to the problem. Indeed, offering bold conjectures seems to be the way of the scientist. That he plays many roles—logician, mathematician, experimentalist, educator—should not allow us to overlook his role as theoretical speculator struggling to learn from experience. Though as yet he has given us little in the way of help in the form of theoretical information concerning problems of learning to read *well,* he has offered us, indirectly, a model for learning. He has offered himself, the scientist, as an exemplar.

But to take him as our model necessitates in many cases a revision of our notions about him. Unlike the Baconian version (*4*), this suggestion asks for the recognition of the scientist as a creative man—as an *abstractor* instead of an *extractor* (*2*). It says that, as man the theoretician, he comes to his work with his theories and he creates theories. Although the scientist as depositary and creator has been played down in the descriptive literature, logic and discretion tell us that it is precisely because he comes with something that he can hope to refine it; for, we cannot refine what we do not have.

The main thesis, then, of this paper is that man the discoverer, man the creator, man the theoretician takes what he has, juggles it, twists it, pulls it and adds to it—sometimes through rearrangement—making interpretation possible.

Taken seriously in the context of reading—especially with the new trend to place rich theoretical information further and further down in the grades—the notion that man is a theoretician means encouraging readers to *boldly conjecture,* to guess. As teachers, it means asking students to prize themselves not as empty storage bins but as theoreticians. To follow such a prescription will increase the incidence of error. It implies that we learn by *making* mistakes. It suggests that teachers help students to become *courageous readers,** readers who are willing to risk mistakes and, going even further, students who are willing to search out their own errors while humbly admitting man's fallibility in the pursuit of learning (*12*).

Of course, there are those who may say that to allow students to think, to wildly guess, may have its dangers. After all, encouragement in

---

*B. E. Cullinan proposed this descriptive label in a private conversation.

the direction I am suggesting may lead to students' prizing their own theories too highly. Like some people whom all of us have known, they may behave, when they first encounter their own ideas, as if this were the first time mankind had ever had them. As offensive as this consequence may seem to some, it tells us that we need to help students to learn *much more*. We need to assist them, for example, in learning to discriminate between questions of *originality* (when, how, and with whom an idea was original) and questions of *status* (whether or not an idea is a "good" one, given the job we want it to do and how we may set about to evaluate it—whoever its inventor).

Learning about Logic and Experimentalism

Asking students to recognize themselves as theoreticians seems to suggest helping them, also, to become logicians and experimentalists. Once students begin to pay attention to their own theories, they will need to find ways to sort them out and to test them. Perforce, they will need to consider, even *as* theoreticians, the problems associated with the quest for knowledge. Questions which they might entertain are: How may we learn from experience? How may we choose hypotheses? and How may we validate theory? This is to say that students should be urged to consider the logic of inquiry.

Were teachers to open this world, students would fast discern how tools of *deductive* logic may be utilized to delineate their speculations in such a way that setting up experiments becomes conceivable. Inventing procedures for testing, when seen as a theoretical activity reserved for the imagination, may become exciting.

Learning to read well seems no exception. The exceptional reader like those distinguished philosophers of whom Russell did *not* complain, to my way of thinking, is a person who is unafraid of his imagination and unafraid of making errors. He is a reader who recognizes ways in which evaluative techniques, such as our evolving rules of logic and methodology, may assist him in garnering interpretations. He does, indeed, want to appreciate the thought of others and actively seeks to come to an understanding of their perspectives and insights—ever aware that their thought, like his, is human and subject to mistakes.

Pioneers in the quest to teach children the use of logic have been many. Teaching children to do so in the circumstances of reading has come to be labeled by educational theorists and researchers "critical" reading (9). Taking their cues from those who have attempted to make analyses of what would constitute "critical thinking" (6), researchers have developed descriptions and exercises whereby teachers might teach and children might learn to make logical and empirical judgments about nonfictional writings.

As important as these contributions have been, they may be, I think, improved through criticism. Let me offer two examples. The first will focus on a situation in which children are taught to judge the warrant of generalizations susceptible to action. The second will focus on teaching children the use of credentials to judge the alleged authority of an expert.

Teaching children rules, through the application of which they may ascertain the reliability of generalizations, hypotheses, conjectures (or systems, thereof), is to teach children a methodology of belief. It is to teach them an answer to the question "How do we know what to believe?" Through the collection of positive cases, children will learn which generalizations are worthy of their belief. In other words, they will learn a means of deciding which generalizations they should act upon. But such generalizations, carrying (at least for children) a high probability of success, quite frankly, may carry a "higher probability" of failure. The reason for this apparent double talk is fairly simple: gross assumptions yield gross predictions. Without highly accurate theoretical information about the behavior of people, generalizations about contemplated actions run a high possibility of error. Even attempts to minimize risk are undercut by the absence of social scientific theory which approximates the truth.

Disillusionment and skepticism may be the outcomes of teaching children to rely on rules of logic which incorporate gross procedures for success (3). When children discover that generalizations gathered from data collection do not work, they may question not only those who teach them the procedures of reasonableness but *reason* itself.

Were this questioning to lead to improved rules for the assessment of hypotheses and not the tragic consequences I have sketched, it would, indeed, constitute a revolution in schooling. It would introduce into our schools the notion that scholars, teachers, and students learn by making mistakes. An innovation of this kind would bring with it the further prescriptions: Make mistakes as fast as you can! And remember them!

Turning to my second example, children may be taught to look up the background or credentials of a writer as an aid to interpreting his work. If children are aware that authors present in their writing their viewpoints or perspectives, they may learn to use information about the author's field, his training, other works he has written, those he footnotes, and so on, as cues for ascertaining his viewpoint. They may, for instance, make hypotheses about the kinds of problems in which scholars or a given discipline are interested and ask of their reading whether these or similar problems are the concern of the author. They may ask whether the problem to which he addresses himself in this work assumes the solution of other problems discussed in his other writings.

What children should *not* be taught is to utilize the credentials of a writer as *some form of guarantee* for his ideas. No matter how many degrees he may hold, how many books he may have written, how high the esteem in which he is held, his theories or ideas (or portions, thereof) may be in error. Although an author may be offering the reader the latest word, *his* latest word, it should *not* be treated as if it were some *guaranteed* word or the *last* word.

While I would opt for the use of logic to assist students in judging the validity of an alleged authority's argument, I would, also, advocate that students be given assistance in learning to play the role of the experimentalist. Teachers could help students to make attempts to determine whether an authority's statements are empirically testable, and, if so, in what ways.

Contriving experimental procedures which count as crucial tests (cases in which there is a strong possibility of refutation) could only broaden a student's perspective of knowledge and the problems associated with its growth. Students should come to see how conflicting viewpoints or theories (if you prefer) aid us in uncovering explanatory deficiencies. Specifically, considering two conflicting theories intended to explain the same phenomenon, they might note observations disclosed by one theory which its competitor must also explain or be labeled deficient. Exploring the subtleties of experimental procedure, they could come to understand "why" statistical generalizations leave room for improvement; to date, we have no adequate means for refuting them (*10, 11*). When we calculate the probabilities of a state of affairs, we are going for the second prize; from the beginning we have admitted that a number of cases will not fall under the *affirmative* scope of our generalization. It is at the point of *application* that "reason" must come into the picture.

One lesson of "reason" is learning that knowledge, like the people who create it, as well as the processes they create for its evaluation, is *human*. And, I can think of no lesson more important to learn or more important to teach. Were educators interested in the social studies to assist the young in learning this lesson, such educators would be far on the way towards shaping a *creative-rational citizenry*.

Appendix: The Logic of Induction

Some among each generation of young philosophers take as their challenge the resolution of the logical problem of induction. These empiricists attempt to find new ways to overcome the skepticism borne of David Hume's (1711-1776) articulation of the dilemma involved in attempting to demonstrate through experience the truth of universal statements. Since universal propositions refer to tomorrow's (infinite) states of affairs, they must refer to unexaminable phenomena—making *complete* empirical demonstration impossible *(4)*. This logical difficulty has vexed, perennially, those who would have science be a system of demonstrably true laws.

A number of approaches have been taken to resolve the empiricists' problem of unjustified inference, i.e., reasoning from the examinable to the unexaminable *(11)*. By far the greatest number of efforts have aimed at crawling over Hume's argument, usually attempting to show its inapplicability. Philosophers of science, in general, have held high hope that Hume was wrong. How else could we explain the unprecedented achievement of science?

The contemporary logician, Sir Karl Popper, has taken a novel approach. Following in the tradition of Immanuel Kant (1724-1804), Popper has accepted what he calls Hume's "logical discovery that induction is irrational" *(11)*. However, he was abandoned, even attacked with logical and empirical arguments *(15)*, Hume's *psychological* thesis that people do and must methodologically induct. Popper points out that the *acquisition of ideas* is a subject for scientific investigation, not a matter of scientific methodology.

Unlike Bertrand Russell, a deductivist who saw a need for inductive inference, Popper has offered a deductive methodology which avoids inductive inference *(16)*. Specifically, it avoids probabilistic and verificationist reasoning. Deductive methodology for Popper amounts to deductive logic (reasoning from the general to the specific) plus negative testing procedures (logical and empirical refutations).

From Popper's standpoint, a body of scientific knowledge may never be demonstrated. Science is a series of *guesses* or *conjectures* which are the result of attempts to formulate and answer scientific problems *(1)*. They are, indeed, guesses and conjectures which have withstood our severest attempts to refute them. But they may never be said to hold greater status —for they are *only man's best approximation* of the truth. Although we may never know the truth, we *may know* what is *not* the truth.

This, it would seem, is a very optimistic viewpoint, for man's *more* creative approximations may lie just around the corner. In fastening on negative experimentalism, efficiency in the growth of knowledge is enhanced. In separating the psychology and sociology of knowledge from its logic and testing, all avenues of acquisition are opened to man's creativity and study.

Popper's studies in logic raise many significant and sticky questions for educators interested in the social studies. Among them are the following:

1. May we be said to be "certain" about theoretical knowledge in any

but the psychological sense that some people feel certain about its truth?

2. If a number of men agree, after careful study of the evidence, that a statement is true, is their judgment only as "good" as their inductive theory of rationality on which it is based?

3. Should "security" in the classroom ever reside, however indirectly, in the knowledge discussed there?

4. Is there a "structure of knowledge" in any sense, save that the formulation of problems is a selection device for the discovery of their solutions?

5. Do theories of induction by repetition and elimination qualify mainly as theories for the inculcation of knowledge?

References

1. Agassi, Joseph. *The Continuing Revolution.* New York: McGraw-Hill, 1968.
2. Agassi, Joseph. "The Novelty of Popper's Philosophy of Science," *International Philosophical Quarterly,* 8 (September 1968), 442-463.
3. Edgerton, Stephanie G. "Have We Really Talked Enough About Authority?" *Studies in Philosophy and Education* (forthcoming).
4. Edgerton, Stephanie G. " 'Learning' By Induction," *Social Education,* 31 (May 1967), 373-376.
5. Ennis, Robert H. "A Concept of Critical Thinking," *Harvard Educational Review,* 32 (Winter 1962), 81-111.
6. Ennis, Robert H. "A Definition of Critical Thinking," *Reading Teacher,* 17 (May 1964), 599-611.
7. Hillary, Edmund. *High Adventure.* New York: E. P. Dutton, 1955.
8. Hillary, Edmund. *No Latitude For Error.* New York: E. P. Dutton, 1961.
9. King, Martha L., Bernice D. Ellinger, and Willavene Wolf (Eds.). *Critical Reading.* Philadelphia: Lippincott, 1967.
10. Korner, S. (Ed.). *Observation and Interpretation in the Philosophy of Physics.* New York: Dover, 1962.
11. Lakatos, Imre (Ed.). *The Problem of Inductive Logic.* Amsterdam: North-Holland, 1968.
12. Perkinson, Henry J. "Fallibilism as a Theory of Instruction," *School Review* (forthcoming).
13. Polanyi, Michael. *Personal Knowledge: Towards a Post-Critical Philosophy* (rev. ed.). New York: Harper and Row, 1964.
14. Polanyi, Michael. *The Tacit Dimension.* London: Routledge and Kegan Paul, 1966.
15. Popper, Karl R. *Conjectures and Refutations.* New York: Basic Books, 1963.
16. Popper, Karl R. *The Logic of Scientific Discovery* (English ed.). New York: Basic Books, 1959.
17. Schilpp, Paul Arthur (Ed.). *The Philosophy of Bertrand Russell,* Vol. 1. New York: Harper and Row, 1966, vii-viii.
18. Taylor, Calvin W., and Frank Barron (Eds.). *Scientific Creativity.* New York: John Wiley and Sons, 1963.